THE ENGLISH

THE MAKING OF A NATION FROM 430 – 1700

MALCOLM BILLINGS

BBC BOOKS

F O R   B R I G I D
W I T H   L O V E

Acknowledgments

A book is never the work of one person; many
people contributed ideas, encouragement and
helped to shape the finished product. My
heartfelt thanks are due to: Christopher Stone
of BBC Radio Features, Arts and Education;
Suzanne Webber and Susan Martineau of BBC
Books; Desmond A. Seal, whose research
provided many original ideas; literary agent
Dinah Wiener; Professor Jonathan Riley-Smith,
Dr Nigel Saul and Dr Pauline Croft of Royal
Holloway and Bedford New College,
University of London; The National Trust,
English Heritage, and the administrators of the
many historic buildings, museums and
institutions in France, Germany, the
Netherlands, Italy and Poland that feature in
The English.

   Brigid, Warwick, Alexia, Henrietta and
Sebastian Billings also generously contributed
much of my time that was due to them.

Published by BBC Books,
a division of BBC Enterprises Limited,
Woodlands, 80 Wood Lane, London W12 0TT
First published 1991
© Malcolm Billings 1991
PB ISBN 0 563 36110 7
HB ISBN 0 563 36114 X
Designed by Harry Green
Maps by Eugene Fleury

Set in Baskerville by Ace Filmsetting Ltd, Frome
Printed and bound in Great Britain by
   Butler and Tanner Ltd, Frome
Jacket and cover printed by Clays Ltd, St Ives plc

Contents

Author's Note

Who are the English? It is a question that many people have attempted to answer. Some have concentrated on historical facts, others on the development of culture. Still others have focused on the character of the English. So far as history is concerned, much more detail has been added to the record in recent years from the exploration of archaeological sites, the study of historic buildings and the discovery, or reassessment, of original manuscripts, with the result that historians have been able to take a fresh look at all aspects of the story of the English.

This book, however, is not another history of the English people. It is, rather, a synthesis of people, places and events. Our focus is on England, and the detailed history of the rest of the British Isles falls beyond the scope of the story I set out to tell. The inspiration for *The English* is drawn not only from historical events, but from the places in which they happened: battlefields; monasteries; castles; medieval new towns; great country houses, and palaces – sites that are often separated or overlooked in the writing of history. I have also become very much aware of England's part in European history. England never was an insular nation.

Wherever possible I have also tried to bring to life the people who lived on the sites that we visit – an outstanding example is Lady Anne Clifford who, in the seventeenth century, ruled her northern estates like a medieval monarch. The characters of such people, the evocation of their lifestyle and the exploration of the places where they lived are at the heart of this book. If this is indeed history, then it is impressionistic and personal. For me it has been a fascinating journey through English history. I am delighted to share it with you.

MALCOLM BILLINGS

Foreword

*I*n making the BBC radio series *The English*, Christopher Stone, the producer, Malcolm Billings and I had to decide what we meant by the 'English'. We opted for the descendants, however intermingled with other races, of the Angles, Saxons and Jutes, and of later settlers, such as the Danes or Normans, who regarded England as their home. The starting point of their history was around AD 430, for it was then that large-scale Anglo-Saxon migration to Britain began. But at what point did the English cease to have a distinctive history? They proved themselves to be aggressive, conquering and colonising Wales and Ireland and trying to conquer Scotland, with the result that perhaps from the twelfth century the histories of the peoples in the British Isles became thoroughly entangled; and from 1603 the kingdoms of England and Scotland were ruled by the same kings. Nevertheless, it seemed to us that the course of events in England had their own particular flavour until constitutional and political union with Scotland in 1707, after which it is impossible to distinguish England from the rest of Great Britain. So 1707 presented itself as a date on which to end; and there was also the fact that early eighteenth-century English culture is close and familiar enough for us to treat its background as our own. Indeed it may be that since 1700, in spite of, or perhaps because of, the Industrial Revolution and population growth and mobility, social attitudes and institutions have tended to preserve cultural elements.

Our earliest experiences when making *The Cross and the Crescent*, a series of BBC radio programmes on the crusades, had convinced Christopher Stone and Malcolm Billings that recording historians at places of historical interest had the effect of heightening their performances through the association of the objects they could see with events in the past. The on-site discussions in *The Cross and the Crescent* had been linked by a commentary, which could make good any deficiencies in the recordings, but it was decided that there would be no linking commentary in *The English*. This imposed on us the discipline of describing what we saw and relating it to the main historical points in conversations of about five minutes' length, which had to fit easily into the sequence of locations that made up each programme. This meant careful planning.

We had also to find a way of crowding nearly 1300 years of history into eight half-hour programmes. That involved breaking the story of the English down into no more than fifty themes or episodes and finding characters which would bring each to life. Although there was not the space to include all topics of importance and my choice could well not be to the taste of everyone, we found a wealth of evocative sites, resonant with English history. Many of them are described in this book.

JONATHAN RILEY-SMITH

CHAPTER ONE

A New Beginning

We must thank a rabbit for directing archaeologists towards the first complete Anglo-Saxon settlement to have been discovered and excavated. In a field alongside the River Lark at West Stow in Suffolk it scratched up fragments of pottery from where they had been left almost 1500 years before by settlers from across the North Sea, who, in time, would call themselves English.

This particular pagan group arrived in about AD 450 to conquer a corner of a landscape that had been farmed by Romanised Britons for generations. The two communities could not have been more different. Only a mile away there was an important Roman settlement with a bath house, batteries of pottery kilns and possibly a Christian church, while the new arrivals, established on a sandy knoll by the river, lived in timber halls and huts. This was to be a new beginning; and, from the fifth century, the English were marked out amongst the Romano-British people they conquered. Ever since, they have developed in ways which can be described as distinctly English – in character, in attitudes, in geography, in government and, perhaps most distinctly of all, in the English language.

This book traces the story of what is called Englishness, and in the company of historian Jonathan Riley-Smith I set out to discover those often indefinable qualities that set the English apart. It was also in our minds to place the English in the context of European experience, and recent investigations have yielded some intriguing results. Through shared traumas of war, invasion, foreign domination, plague, and political and religious upheaval, that which is uniquely English is our theme. To explore it, and to build up the jigsaw, we visit many of the most important sites in English history, some well known, others less so, both in England and abroad.

Our story ends around 1700, with the Industrial Revolution and the Act of Union which created Great Britain. But by then the English are the English. Their character is recognisable to us, we can understand their speech and we can understand their writings. With them, English people of today share more than twelve centuries of collective experience, an experience that begins, for us, in villages such as West Stow.

What we know about Anglo-Saxon domestic life has only recently come to light. Because the Anglo-Saxons built with wood, much of the evidence of their settlements literally rotted away. However, in the case of West Stow, the excavators were lucky. In the soil, archaeologists uncovered the faint stains of rotted wood from posts that had been dug into the ground to support timber frames and thatched roofs. Regular lines of post holes show the shape of the buildings. And today you get an uncanny feeling of visiting fifth-century England as you walk among thatched houses, and a hen house, that archaeologists have reconstructed exactly where they stood all those centuries ago.

The first English village consisted of groups of buildings each with a central hall and up to a dozen or so smaller huts scattered around it. Had it not been for a capricious act of nature none of this might have been known. Some time in the Middle Ages, well after the site had been abandoned, sand began to build up over the fields of West Stow and covered the landscape with a protective blanket. Post holes, hearths, charred wood from burnt-out houses and everyday household items were left there, undisturbed.

It is clear from the Roman items found around the village – coins and pottery in large quantities – that the Anglo-Saxons and their neighbours co-existed for some time, but how they rubbed along together is, unfortunately, not part of the archaeological record. There is no doubt, however, about the origin of these people. They had, for us, the fortunate habit of burying family heirlooms with their dead; and in the cemetery, about 300 metres from the village, brooches, weapons and pottery have established clear links with archaeological sites in the Anglo-Saxon homelands north of the Rhine.

These were the people who, by the end of the seventh century, had settled and apparently dominated all of south-east England, the Midlands, East Anglia and the eastern half of northern England. What inspired them to cross the sea, and how they came to dominate the well-rooted culture of the Romano-British, is still being debated by historians and archaeologists.

What we do know is that these people spoke a form of English. We would not recognise it as such if we were to hear it but already English was an intensely poetic and powerful language. Thirty thousand lines of early English poetry survive, and that language which expressed the developing culture was even able to outlast later centuries of domination by a foreign-speaking aristocracy. Walking around West Stow at dusk we had no difficulty imagining one of the central halls, lit only by the glow of a fire and a few guttering lamps, with the whole community gathered to hear heroic poetry and to tell stories of magic and tradition.

Britain was invaded by Frisians from around the Zuider Zee and the Frisian Islands, Saxons from along the estuary of the Weser in northern Germany, and Angles and Jutes who shared the Jutland peninsula, with the latter dominating the northern end.

West Stow Anglo-Saxon Village

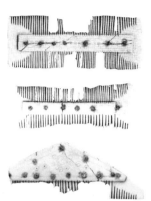

Left: *Bone combs made from several bone plates held together with layers of flat pieces cut from red deer antler. Iron rivets secure all the pieces.*

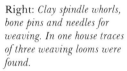

Right: *Clay spindle whorls, bone pins and needles for weaving. In one house traces of three weaving looms were found.*

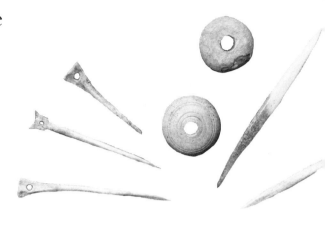

During excavations between 1965 and 1972 the remains of two main types of buildings were clear enough for archaeologists to reconstruct one of the central halls and several smaller houses using the original post holes. The halls were up to 12 metres long with a door in the south side and a central hearth. The houses, about 4 metres long, had walls made of planks and were built over rectangular pits with two or three posts at either end to support a pitched roof. There is clear evidence that the houses had planked floors and clay hearths and that the Anglo-Saxons were not living a semi-troglodyte existence in squalid pits as historians thought until recently. Some of the houses must have been used as workshops – there were traces of three weaving looms in one – and iron slag found on the site indicates that a smithy had been at work.

The village was probably paying its way in the world with grain, hides and wool. In what must have been seen as conspicuous consumption, someone in the village was evidently fond of exotic sea shells. A giant cowrie shell that probably came from the Red Sea was found in a rubbish pit. By the mid-seventh century West Stow was fading away as families moved from their village with a view over the water meadows to another site along the river where the soil might have been more productive and where a Christian church had been built.

Until the excavations, the town of Bury St Edmunds had earmarked the site as a council rubbish dump, but that planning decision was reversed and the ancient Anglo-Saxon village has been developed as a unique Country Park where the reconstructed houses, a visitors' centre and demonstrations of metal- and wood-working create a lasting image of life in Anglo-Saxon England.

These Anglo-Saxons were no strangers to Roman Britain. Their ancestors had been harrying the Romans for at least 200 years. In their homelands these 'barbarians' had made a living out of raiding Roman settlements, not only along the British coast but in Gaul as well. Their evolution from piracy to settlement, however, takes us back into a period in which records are sparse and speculation rife.

The 'Saxon Shore'

We do know that the Anglo-Saxons were such a menace that the Romans called the east and south coasts of Britain the 'Saxon Shore' and in the late third century, between AD 270 and AD 285, a string of fortresses, such as Pevensey, Richborough and Portchester, stretching from the Wash to Portsmouth, was needed to protect the coast. Surveying the scene today from the

Bronze cruciform brooches with a spring fastening, decorated with animal, bird and human masks. The ornate one is from the late fifth century and the plain one from a century later. The brooches, which came from the cemetery near the village, closely resemble those found in cemeteries in northern Germany and southern Denmark.

Below: *West Stow Anglo-Saxon Village.*

walls of Portchester Castle in Portsmouth Harbour, it is easy to see how an Anglo-Saxon ship trying to slip into one of the estuaries would have been easily spotted and the Roman Channel Fleet, based at Dover, alerted by a series of beacons. The fourth-century Roman writer, Vegetius, sounding like a contributor to *Jane's Fighting Ships*, describes 'scouting vessels attached to the battle cruisers' as if they were part of the Royal Navy's World War II Special Boat Operations. 'Sails and rigging alike are painted a dark sea-blue colour so that ships do not give themselves away. Even the wax they use to caulk their vessels is dyed.'

But the fleet and the forts of the Saxon Shore failed to hold the line. Roman Britain was under attack from all sides: the Irish, confusingly called 'Scots' from 'Scotia' (the late-Roman word for Ireland), raided and settled where they could along the west coast; and from the area of Strathclyde the Picts kept the Hadrian's Wall garrison on its toes. For as long as the Roman army did its job – at times there were as many as 50 000 troops stationed in the province – the barbarian threat could be contained. But towards the end of the fourth century the core of the Roman Empire came under pressure, and in AD 410 Rome itself fell.

As for Britain, for some time troops had been removed to fight elsewhere in the Empire under a soldier who declared himself emperor. But the pressures from the barbarians increased and the British leaders sent envoys with appeals for help. They went unheeded and, with the fall of Rome, Honorius, the legitimate Emperor, made it clear to the Romano-British that there was nothing that the imperial government could do for them; with a letter from the Emperor to that effect, almost four centuries of Roman rule in Britain ended in confusion.

🌿

Only one writer sheds much light on what happened – the British priest Gildas who lived in the north-west of Britain in the first half of the sixth century. After Roman rule had been abandoned he writes that 'loathsome hordes of Scots and Picts eagerly emerged from the coracles that carried them across the gulf of the sea like dark swarms of worms'. Gildas paints a picture of mayhem and misery as Christian communities, extremely sinful in his view, were attacked and slaughtered. He also provides us with a date which helps to place the beginning of Anglo-Saxon settlement in England. He describes 'the miserable remnants' of Roman Britain as sending a letter to the imperial authorities: 'to Agitius (Aetius), consul for the third time, come the groans of the Britons . . . the barbarians drive us into the sea; the sea drives us to the barbarians; between these two means of death we are either killed or drowned'. Aetius was the Western Empire's commander-in-chief. His third consulship began in AD 446, and that date provided

by Gildas is perhaps the last fixed point in the chronology of post-Roman Britain.

The 'groans of the Britons' would have been passed on to the Emperor who, by this time, was ruling from the comparative safety of Ravenna on the Adriatic coast of northern Italy. Some of fifth- and sixth-century Ravenna survives today, tucked away in a network of narrow medieval and Renaissance streets. Most notable are the Cathedral of San Vitale, where the interior walls are covered with marble and mosaic, and the small, cruciform mausoleum of the Empress Galla Placidia, decorated almost entirely with mosaics. Entering these buildings is one way of coming closer to the ancient empire of which Britain was a part, and from which it was so reluctantly parted.

Portchester Castle's Roman wall and bastions; the Norman castle keep.

Portchester Castle

Anyone who believes that there is hardly anything of Roman Britain surviving above knee height should be delighted at the sight of Portchester Castle. All the walls and many of the turrets still stand to their full height of 5.5 metres, and at ground level you can see the original thickness of about 3 metres. The Solent still laps the walls and, standing on the ramparts, you get the same view right down to the harbour that the Roman lookouts would have had 1600 years ago. The flint, tile and stone walls form an almost perfect square and English Heritage claims that there is no better preserved Roman fort of its kind in northern Europe. Of course, the original wooden Roman military barracks have not survived and the fortress has inevitably acquired later buildings which make the site even more interesting. Within the Roman walls is a Norman castle (centre). In the south-west corner (bottom centre) a fine Romanesque church, left over from the Augustinian priory established in 1139, is still used as a parish church.

The castle was remodelled by Richard II, who built the palace adjoining the keep which today survives as an impressive, echoing ruin. Excavation in the 1960s showed that an 'English' foothold was established here in the early 500s: a Saxon settlement that lasted for several generations at the time when warrior leaders were carving kingdoms for themselves out of post-Roman Britain.

The Roman wall with fourteen of its twenty original rounded bastions intact. Some of those missing may have been undermined by the sea.

Mausoleum of Galla Placidia

In this building there is no sense of an empire beset by danger on all sides. The Mausoleum of Galla Placidia, the best preserved example of Ravenna's fifth-century architecture, was built just before the last British plea for help arrived and its lavishly decorated interior has some of the most beautiful mosaics from the Roman world. Scrolls of foliage, geometric patterns and biblical scenes cover almost every inch of the walls and ceilings. One group, with full-length figures dressed in purple-bordered tunics and voluminous cloaks embroidered with gold lettering, portrays the sartorial style of the courtiers at Ravenna in AD 446. The alabaster windows let through a soft, diffused light that barely reaches the superb mosaics on the vaulted ceilings and elegant dome, so well-prepared visitors arm themselves with coins for the floodlight slot machine. For a few short minutes the interior bursts into brilliant colour with mosaic tapestries depicting fountains, doves and pastoral scenes in blues, browns, greens, reds and gold that almost take your breath away.

Galla Placidia, the sister of Emperor Honorius and the mother of Valentinian II, was never interred in the mausoleum. She was buried in Rome in AD 450 and it was not until the early Middle Ages that the three sarcophagi we see today were moved here.

During the Renaissance it was said that the Empress's body could be seen sitting upright in a chair of cypress wood; but, the story goes, a gang of inquisitive boys in 1557 put lighted candles through a hole in the tomb and set the wood on fire, destroying everything except a few bones and fragments of wood. The other two sarcophagi have also been opened but their contents revealed nothing of the history of the original occupants.

The British appeal to the Empire in the mid-fifth century failed like all the others. The result was a change of strategy in Britain. According to Gīldas, 'the proud tyrant' Vortigern, who had emerged as a national leader, responded to the barbarian emergency by hiring some of the 'fierce Saxons' as mercenaries. Horsa and Hengist were two of these mercenaries. It was the beginning of the end. The Venerable Bede, writing in the eighth century, tells us that they brought their people 'in three long ships, and were granted land in the eastern part of the island'. Bede's dating of this event, AD 449, fits in with the date of Anglo-Saxon cemeteries in the south and east of England, although some burials can be dated by their grave goods to the first part of the fifth century.

Among the British leaders we so faintly hear about in the fifth and sixth centuries there is one outstanding omission – Arthur. He is missing from Gildas's contemporary account, and references to anyone called Arthur are sparse in the other source material. A Welsh ninth-century annal says that there was a military commander, not a king, called Arthur at Mount Badon – a site in southern England, now lost to historians – and

The interior of the Mausoleum of Galla Placidia showing the three mysterious marble sarcophagi. Above the middle sarcophagus, once thought to contain the Empress's body, is the figure believed to be that of St Lawrence preparing for his martyrdom; in the lunette above, two full-size figures are wearing the attire of fifth-century Roman courtiers.

Below: *The Mausoleum of Galla Placidia, Ravenna, built in AD 440.*

ern Britain, but beyond that we know very little about him. In a single reference, Bede calls him King Cerdic, but the *Anglo-Saxon Chronicle*, a collection of early writings put together in the ninth century and continued until after the Norman invasion, tells us that he landed in AD 494 and was the founder of a dynasty that was to rule the new English kingdom of Wessex. It is clear that Cerdic had impeccable pagan credentials. His genealogy is traced from the great god Woden! Yet in Cerdic we see the essential ambiguity of the English which is at the heart of Englishness.

The first king of Wessex, and therefore the progenitor of the present royal family, had a British name – Cerdic – and although he fought alongside the Anglo-Saxons (the embryonic English) he may not have been English himself. He could have been the son of a Saxon father

another annal records the death of an Arthur at the Battle of Camlann in AD 537; and that is about all we know. Arthur, as he is portrayed today, with knights, round table and heroic escapades, is a character from the medieval imagination conjured up by the twelfth-century 'historian' Geoffrey of Monmouth.

Another warrior from that time is Cerdic. Jonathan Riley-Smith painted a picture of that enigmatic character as we explored Portchester Castle. He won a kingdom for himself in south-

Kingdoms, towns and important sites in about AD 600.

and a British mother. He could have been a Briton from Brittany, which had already been settled by many Romano-British escaping from the Anglo-Saxons. He may have been an apostate and a renegade, a Christian Romano-Briton who had abandoned his home, his people and his faith, and returned leading a pirate band. We do not know. But what we do know is that, for a large part of our story, Britain was not isolated from the continent. There was quite extraordinary international movement going on even then.

The new settlers are thought to have maintained strong links with the Franks across the North Sea, whose frontiers in the sixth and seventh centuries incorporated most of what is now modern France, along with Switzerland, Germany and Belgium. We know from the 'omniscient' Bede that the pagan king, Aethelbert (560–616), married a Frankish Christian princess in the second half of the sixth century; and there are hints in contemporary Roman sources about Anglo-Saxons returning to the continent to settle among the Franks.

These Anglo-Saxon contacts with continental Europe and countries beyond are nowhere better demonstrated than in the grave of an East Anglian king at Sutton Hoo in Suffolk. His ship burial, in a sandy, bracken-covered field, was discovered just before the outbreak of war in 1939, complete with a hoard of jewellery, silver plate and personal effects for his journey to the other world. Archaeological evidence certainly suggests that the king was Redwald. With him, as we saw when we visited the permanent exhibition in the British Museum, he took a mass of goods needed for the afterlife. We were staggered by the craftsmanship. To describe such treasures as the work of 'barbarians' gives a completely false idea of the richness, and the geographical extent, of Saxon culture.

Sutton Hoo Treasure

The ship and the body were missing when excavators in 1939 dug into one of the burial mounds overlooking the River Deben in Suffolk. The timbers of the ship, 27 metres long, had gone completely and only their impression was left in the soft, damp sand. All the rusted rivets, however, were still in position so it was possible for archaeologists to make a plaster cast of the ship and reproduce it for display. When the ship was first uncovered, and its remarkable treasure emerged, no sign of a body could be found.

It was many years before scientific analysis of the sand in the ship revealed telltale phosphates, indicating that a body had lain among the treasure. The king's sword, for fighting alongside the great god Woden, had a jewelled gold pommel and hilt; his shield's iron boss and metal fittings were decorated with designs of birds, animal heads and dragons with garnet eyes; silver bowls and a richly decorated plate came from the best craftsmen in the Byzantine empire. The king's reconstructed helmet still has an aura of the power once wielded by its wearer.

The king's purse, inlaid with garnets and millefiori glass, contained gold coins from mints throughout the Frankish kingdom – payment, perhaps, for the forty ghostly oarsmen needed to row the vessel on its final voyage to the mythical Valhalla. The coins, in fact, turned out to be the only clue to the identity of the occupant of the grave. They could not have been brought together earlier than 625 and, according to Bede's genealogy of the East Anglian royal house, Redwald was the most likely contender for this remarkable burial. As we look at Redwald's grave goods in the British Museum today, our twentieth-century perception of the early Anglo-Saxon kings is overturned. 'Barbarian' quickly seems an inappropriate description. The mound that was heaped up over the ship and its contents bears an uncanny resemblance to a ship burial described in that famous Anglo-Saxon epic poem *Beowulf*, written in England about 700:

'Then the Geats built a barrow on the headland –
it was high and broad, visible from far
to all seafarers; in ten days they built the beacon
for that courageous man; and they constructed
as noble an enclosure as wise men
could devise, to enshrine the ashes.
They buried rings and brooches in the barrow,
all those adornments that brave men
had brought out from the hoard after Beowulf died.
They bequeathed the gleaming gold, treasure of men,
to the earth, and there it was before.
Then twelve brave warriors, sons of heroes,
rode round the barrow, sorrowing;
they mourned their king, chanted
an elegy, spoke about that great man:
They exalted his heroic life, lauded
his daring deeds.'

Reconstruction of the badly corroded and shattered iron helmet. It closely resembles helmets found in Swedish ship burials; its bronze eyebrows are inlaid with silver wires and end in a small gilt bronze boar's head.

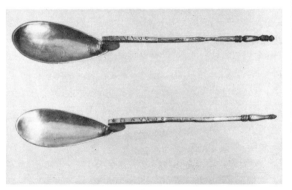

Large classical silver spoons that Redwald might have received at his baptism; the names 'Saul' and 'Paul' are inscribed in Greek on the handles.

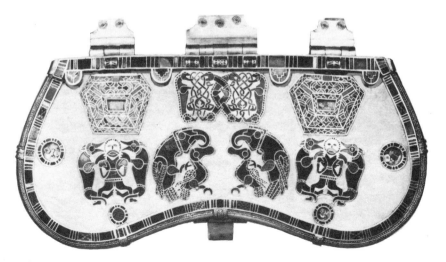

Garnets and millefiori glass in a gold frame decorate the lid of the king's purse. The lid which has been reconstructed was probably made of bone or ivory.

By the time of Redwald's death in 624 or 625, Christianity had been reintroduced into pagan England by St Augustine, and Redwald may have been among the saint's early converts. Although Bede confirms that Redwald was baptised, the pagan warrior apparently had second thoughts, so the Christian items found in his otherwise pagan grave, such as the pair of silver christening spoons and silver bowls decorated with a cross, were perhaps a hedge against a future tinged with doubt.

Conversion to Christianity

St Augustine's mission, nevertheless, was to have a profound effect on England; and from Bede we know the very place where the conversion of the English began: St Martin's Church in Canterbury. It was a strange feeling, walking in the church where Christianity, such an influence on the story of the English, first returned to England. Bede says it was 'an old church built in honour of St Martin during the Roman occupation of Britain where the Christian Queen Bertha of whom I have spoken went to pray'. There are good reasons to believe that St Martin's Church was indeed the one given to the Christian princess and her chaplain when she came to Canterbury to marry King Aethelbert in the late sixth century, and that the same building served as St Augustine's headquarters at the start of his mission in 597. Roman and Anglo-Saxon buildings, as we could see for ourselves quite plainly, had been integrated into later developments.

Converting the English turned out to be hard work for the forty members of Augustine's mission. Even King Aethelbert was chary about its intentions. It is said, for example, that the king, when he met Augustine for the first time, refused

St Martin's, Canterbury

In many ways St Martin's is typical of any parish church, with its medieval and nineteenth-century work. Some parishes may boast Saxon walls or foundations, but few offer upstanding Roman walls. Excavations at the end of the nineteenth century revealed that the earliest part of the church is made of Roman brick, typical of the fourth century. But church archaeologist Tim Tatton-Brown believes that the original Roman building could have been a Christian mausoleum in the form of a shrine, in Roman Canterbury's cemetery, outside the city wall. One tantalising find in St Martin's churchyard was a small hoard of coins, including one which bore the name of Liuhard – Queen Bertha's chaplain. The walls of the nave are also made of Roman brick with 'pink' mortar. These walls use the brick as string courses in between rows of sandstone blocks. This suggests a post-Roman technique, but experts agree that the nave could not have been built later than the seventh century.

Bede tells us that Augustine built a new church – the first Canterbury Cathedral – and from the porch of St Martin's we looked out on the medieval towers of its successor. It is not difficult to believe that St Martin's predated the first cathedral, and Christian services have been held in that little parish church for almost 1400 years without a break.

to talk to him indoors for fear of the magic that the saint may have brought from Rome. The missionaries approached the king, chanting and carrying a silver cross and a picture of Jesus painted on a wooden board. Aethelbert allowed them to preach and was eventually won over to become the first of the Christian English kings. Others followed but, like Redwald, were not entirely steadfast in their conversion, and at one stage the missionaries almost gave up.

Travelling to London along the A2, which follows substantially the line of the Roman Watling Street, we saw evidence of the early successes of

Above: *South wall of the chancel of St Martin's Church. The string courses of brick are Roman work typical of the late fourth century. The round-headed window is a later addition to a building that may once have been a Roman Christian tomb.*

St Martin's Church where the Christian Queen Bertha is thought to have worshipped when she came from France to marry Aethelbert in the last quarter of the sixth century. Legend has it that the East Anglian pagan king Redwald was baptised here.

the mission, only to remember that the bishops of Rochester and London were actually driven out of their churches and had to flee to France after Aethelbert died in 616. But Christianity had a foothold in England and the mission was given a boost of confidence when the Northumbrian King Edwin married a Christian in 615. His queen came from the royal family of Kent and together with Paulinus, her chaplain, she converted King Edwin in 617: 'with all the nobility of his kingdom and a large number of humbler folk, he accepted the faith and they were washed with the cleansing water of baptism'.

Bede also tells us that the Celtic Christian Church was just as active in the conversion of the heathen English, and from the monastery established at Lindisfarne off the north-east coast by the Irish missionary Aidan, monks carried the gospel south into the Midlands and East Anglia. By the time that the Venerable Bede entered his monastery at Jarrow in the north-east in the early 680s, the conflict between the Celtic and the Roman Church had been largely resolved by the Synod of Whitby, and Archbishop Theodore of Canterbury had led his expanded and re-organised Church into a golden age.

Christianity was in England to stay and the influence of the Church on English history and character is one we shall trace throughout this book. But the coming of Christianity to England also highlighted another aspect of Englishness – the way in which an idea, once accepted, can spread with astounding speed. In only ninety years the Anglo-Saxons embraced the Christian culture with as much enthusiasm as they had swamped the legacy of Romano-British traditions. Literacy and learning returned to England augmenting the Anglo-Saxons' superb sense of design and craftsmanship. You can see that coming through in the eighth-century manuscripts, written at monasteries such as Jarrow. Latin texts imaginatively illuminated echo the artistry of the master craftsmen who worked for Redwald in the sixth and seventh centuries.

England's reputation as a centre of Christian culture in northern Europe began to emerge with the career of the Venerable Bede, whose great historical work has already told us so much about the development of England. He entered the monastery at Monkwearmouth as a young boy in about 680 and two years later moved into the community's new monastery at Jarrow on the south bank of the River Tyne. Bede's prolific output included books about spelling, natural history, the art of writing verse and the lives of the saints, and, at the age of fifty-nine, he

Bede's Monastery, Jarrow

The chancel of the present church of St Paul at Jarrow dates from 681 and is a building that Bede himself would have known. But today it is surrounded by grim industrial sites. The distant whirring and clanking of the docks on the Tyne add another discordant note, so the auguries for a rewarding contact with Bede are not good. However, once inside the churchyard, modern Jarrow does not impinge and walking around the south side of the chancel the first thing you see are three small round windows high up in the wall. There is no doubt that they were glazed by the monks or by craftsmen brought in from Italy or France. The evidence for this has come from Professor Rosemary Cramp's excavation of the monastery buildings, where many fragments of clear and coloured glass were recovered. That such early churches in England had glazed windows was a revelation in itself. No other example of Saxon window glass has ever been found in England.

Bede's monastery was levelled when the Normans rebuilt Jarrow in the eleventh century and, in the excavations, from under the Norman ruins emerged

Bede, as he was depicted in a later medieval manuscript of his Life of St Cuthbert.

embarked on his most famous work, *The History of the English Church and People*. Indeed, he laid the foundations for English history as, up to the last few years before his death in 735, he sought out ancient and contemporary writings and oral traditions ranging from 55 BC to his own lifetime.

Although Sir Gilbert Scott's Victorian hand can be discerned in the present church of St Paul at Jarrow, there is still a remarkable amount of Anglo-Saxon work for us to see. It emphasises the importance of this place, as Jonathan Riley-Smith pointed out. Monastic and palace libraries all over Europe wanted Bede's history, and it was still being copied by hand in the fifteenth century. In his lifetime Bede was considered to be

A page from Bede's famous Bible called the **Codex Amiatinus**. *It is the oldest complete Latin Bible and is now in the Laurentian Library, Florence. The skins of 500 calves would have been needed to make this Bible, which weighs some 30 kilograms.*

St Paul's Church, Jarrow, site of the Venerable Bede's seventh-century monastery.

the outline of the eighth-century refectory, some 30 metres long and with a small room at one end. The floors were made in the Roman way with concrete and chips of red brick, and the walls were plastered. Another fascinating find in what is left of the two-storey refectory building was the remains of a stone desk, found in such a position that it may have been used for scripture readings while the monks took

their meals. Small metal instruments, used to mark out vellum, were found among some of the monks' personal possessions, which included bone combs, pendant-like whetstones for sharpening knives and sinkers made of stone for fishing in what were then the pure waters of the River Tyne. The finds are all on display in the elegant rooms of a Georgian house that overlooks the site.

Charlemagne's Chapel

the most learned man in Europe. That may seem an extravagant claim for an English monk who never travelled beyond the north of England, but it is true, for Bede's vast knowledge had come from a monastery library that was second to none. Jarrow's founder, Benedict Biscop, who had made five trips to Rome, had come back laden with books, great tomes of vellum sometimes weighing over 30 kilograms, each made from the skins of at least 500 calves. The logistics of transporting such items across Europe must have been formidable. But the Anglo-Saxons seemed to take it in their stride; the North Sea and the English Channel were considered highways towards Europe and the East rather than barriers to travel.

Monasteries like Jarrow also provided the intellectual manpower for missions to convert the pagan peoples of northern Europe. The English, so recently pagans themselves, set out to evangelise their kinsmen across the North Sea and were remarkably successful. As early as 676 the Northumbrian bishop, St Wilfrid, on his way to Rome, spent about six months among the Frisian Islanders where he managed to convert their king. A permanent mission followed, led by St Willibrord, one of Wilfrid's students. The names of these two Anglo-Saxons are more familiar in the Low Countries and in Germany today than they are to most people in England.

Another well-known Englishman who took the Gospel to the European mainland was Boniface. He was educated at the monasteries of Exeter and Nursling, and went on to help to reform the Church in Bavaria. Later, he was invited to do the same for the Church in the Frankish kingdom. When Charlemagne became Emperor of the Western Roman Empire in 800 it was to an

Above: *The shrine containing the remains of Charlemagne. It is an oak chest with panels covered with silver and gold figures.*

Left: *The royal throne on which according to tradition Charlemagne was crowned; between 936 and 1531 twenty-nine German kings used the throne during their coronations.*

Between 790 and 800 Charlemagne's magnificent new chapel began to take shape in his palace at Aachen (Aix-la-Chapelle). Alcuin might have seen some of the building materials arrive from Ravenna – marble columns taken out of buildings that belonged to the last of the Roman emperors. Charlemagne clearly saw himself as their natural heir well before his coronation and the chapel's resemblance to the sixth-century church of San Vitale in imperial Ravenna is surely no coincidence.

Charlemagne's chapel, however, is smaller and the outer wall of the rotunda has sixteen sides. Inside, the walls are lined with marble and a double tier of galleries is topped by a mosaic-covered cupola. High up on the first-floor gallery you can see a marble throne reputed to be Charlemagne's own, but there is no doubt about the claim that between 936 and 1531 twenty-nine German kings mounted the five steps to the simple slab-sided throne after they had been consecrated and crowned at the altar.

When the chapel was under construction, Charlemagne had a collection of relics brought from Jerusalem, including the garment worn by Mary on the night of Christ's birth, and the cloth used at the beheading of John the Baptist. They are now in the cathedral treasury, but in the Middle Ages the crush of people wanting to see them was so great that an extension to the chapel was built. Its slender pillars, which soar almost 30 metres to a delicate rib-vaulted ceiling, divide such great expanses of windows that the additional chapel was known as the 'Glass House of Aachen'. In the centre of the floor Charlemagne's gold-covered feretory, or shrine, illuminated by a spotlight from above, leaves today's pilgrims with an unforgettable impression of 'Dark Age' splendour.

English scholar, Alcuin, that he turned for advice and learning.

Charlemagne, Europe's most powerful ruler for 400 years, invited Alcuin to take over the Palace School at Aachen. As Master, he led a revival of learning and art. The palace chapel is now all that remains of the complex of buildings, but it is quite magnificent. With other buildings on the same scale, life there in the eighth and ninth centuries must have been a grand affair for the lucky ones. Alcuin gathered around him some of the best scholars of the time, including many of his former pupils from York, and for more than twenty years he was the Frankish ruler's chief adviser on Church matters, and on dealings with the English kings. His influence on the Frankish Empire was immense. When he died in 804 at the Abbey of St Martin of Tours, Alcuin left a legacy of learning and scholarship that could be compared with that of the Venerable Bede. But before he died the English at home had themselves to face a pagan invasion from across the North Sea that threatened to snuff out all the achievements of Anglo-Saxon culture.

The Emperor Charlemagne's Palace Chapel, Aachen, Germany. Completed in 805, it is the only church commissioned by Charlemagne to survive in what was the Holy Roman Empire. Among the many treasures of the cathedral is a piece of English medieval royal regalia – the dove-topped sceptre of Richard of Cornwall, Henry III's brother who was crowned King of the Romans.

CHAPTER TWO

Anglo-Saxon Civilisation

Standing in a Viking settlement at Haithabu, better known by its Danish name of Hedeby, in northern Germany and looking down to the harbour, it was not difficult for Jonathan Riley-Smith and myself to call to mind the fierce-looking longboats of the eighth and ninth centuries. 'Never before has such a terror appeared in Britain as we have now suffered from a pagan race.' Alcuin, writing after the first Viking raid in 793, was as shocked as any Englishman. Although tribal warfare was endemic in an England peppered with territorially jealous kings, the Vikings were a new menace that rose out of the sea without warning. They ransacked, they looted and they slipped away before the English could muster any defence.

And their impact on England was profound. Lindisfarne was an obvious target. Vulnerable to Viking attacks, it was an island off the north-east coast where Irish monks had founded a monastery, and where St Cuthbert had been prior in 664. Lindisfarne's church, 'splattered with blood of the priests of God', was the first recorded casualty on the English coast. Bede's monastery at Jarrow was attacked the following year and, as word spread that English Christian churches were stacked with portable riches, no coastal community was beyond the reach of the ferocious longboats.

From their homelands in Denmark, Norway and Sweden the Vikings targeted the entire western seaboard of Europe. The Frisian trading settlement at the mouth of the Rhine was only one casualty. Dorestad, Hamburg, Paris and Nantes were also attacked, and cities as far south

Hedeby

The high earthen ramparts that arc around the site, enclosing about 27½ hectares, are the sole remains of Hedeby above ground, but if you follow the path along their top you come to a new museum which overlooks the sea. The museum gardens have been planted with species of plants and trees that the archaeological excavation tells us grew there in Viking times. The museum has all the most important finds since excavations began at Hedeby in the early 1900s: amber rings, beads and gaming pieces; lathes for polishing and shaping jewellery; moulds made out of bone, clay, stone and wood for casting metal; and 6824 carefully counted glass beads manufactured on the site. From other parts of the world, silk, pottery and high-grade metal goods were brought by Viking traders along Europe's great river systems. The very successful import/export business revealed at Hedeby answers a question that has bothered historians for generations. It was international trade that financed the great Danish armies that marched at such cost up and down England!

Personal items found in the excavations give us some idea of what these people might have looked like as they walked among the rows of thatched houses on corrugated streets made of rafts of logs: the men wore woollen tunics or baggy trousers with leggings and perhaps a cloak with a metal shoulder clasp, and the women ankle-length tunics or skirts. On special occasions, the women wore embroidered silk and linen pleated shirts with a slit neck. Their garments sparkled with gold and silver thread, and fur trimmings added another touch of luxury. The image we have of a Dark Age people in dreary colours is far from the truth – their clothes were dyed in an array of bright greens, browns and reds. We know so much about Hedeby's wardrobe because of what was found at the bottom of the harbour. When the ships needed tarring the 'maintenance men' used bundles of old clothes as paint brushes, and along with remains of ships themselves, archaeologists found the tar-soaked clothes preserved in the harbour silts. The timbers

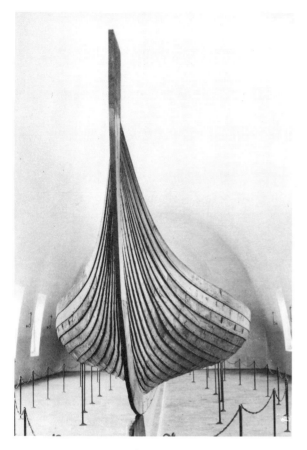

Left: *Prow of the Gokstad ship excavated from a burial mound near Oslo in 1881. Over 23 metres long, it could carry 50 to 60 warriors.*

Above: *Hedeby's earthern ramparts once enclosed a thriving Viking trading centre. The museum houses all the finds from the town and harbour.*

Silver coins for payment were weighed in scales. Coins found at Hedeby originated from all over Scandinavia and Central Europe.

A brooch typical of those cast from lead and bronze. Moulds of antler bone, clay or stone could be used for mass production.

they discovered were from a warship, a trading vessel and a flat-bottomed barge, all of which have provided enough evidence to attempt reconstruction drawings and models.

The international reach of the Vikings was only made possible through the development of the perfect sailing machine. The Gokstad ship, for example, excavated from a burial mound near Oslo in 1881, was made of single oak planks that were over 23 metres long with a beam of more than 5 metres. Her big square sail could push her across the open sea at about 10 knots with fifty or sixty armed warriors on board. Given names like 'Racing Serpent', the longboats were designed to bend in a seaway and remain watertight on a North Sea crossing. A draught of only a metre made them ideal for beaching and for slipping into estuaries and rivers to surprise inland settlements.

as Seville experienced the terror of Viking raids. And it was Viking warriors, led by Rollo, who settled at the mouth of the Seine at the beginning of the tenth century and who are credited with the foundation of the Duchy of Normandy – such an important name in the later story of the English. The square sails and carved prows of Viking longboats had carried their warrior crews to plunder towns and cities around the Black Sea, and to attack Constantinople, the capital of the Byzantine empire. Iceland was already settled and the epic voyages to Greenland and North America were soon to come.

It is hardly surprising that this eruption of pagan sea-power should have been viewed unfavourably by the Anglo-Saxon chroniclers, who saw only churches put to the torch and Christians taken away to be sold into slavery. However, archaeologists and historians have begun to refocus our image of the Vikings by revealing their skills as craftsmen, designers and colonisers, and, above all, as the creators of an international trading network.

The Viking Trade Route

All these facets of the Viking character we could appreciate for ourselves at Hedeby. This oldest of Scandinavian towns goes back to the early ninth century when rows of wooden houses and roadways made of logs began to appear on the shore of one of the Baltic's many inlets.

Archaeologists began to excavate Hedeby's Dark Age past in the early 1900s, but it is only in the last twenty-five to thirty years that the network of trading posts, of which Hedeby was the terminus, has come to light. And through the archaeological sites and the traded goods unearthed, historians have traced the trade route back along the Dvina and Dniepr rivers to the Black Sea and along the Volga to the Caspian Sea.

Via this route trade from the East flowed across Europe. And from Hedeby it went on as far as the Viking settlements on the Isle of Man and Dublin.

The *Anglo-Saxon Chronicle*, a series of annals compiled in the late ninth century and continued through the Norman invasions, says that the Danish conquest of England had begun in earnest with the arrival of 'the great heathen army' which landed in East Anglia in 865. We learn that the Vikings 'were supplied with horses and that the Angles made peace with them'. But once the eastern part of the country had been subdued, the army made its way north, crossed the Humber and fought its way into York – the capital of the kingdom of Northumbria. Here, we understand, the Northumbrian King Aelle suffered the Viking rite of 'blood eagle' in which the victim's lungs and ribs were cut from the living flesh and spread out like the wings of an eagle, as an offering to Odin.

The Danes chose to settle inside the Roman walls of York. This came to light when, in the late 1970s, a large swathe of York was being redeveloped. One of the streets involved was Coppergate and archaeologists, working on the site before construction work began, came across the remains of a row of four Viking houses. What they found in and around the buildings revealed a thriving Danish settlement – a town of many times the population of Hedeby and clearly part of the Vikings' international trading network.

Nothing like this had ever been found in England before and York seized the opportunity to preserve and display a unique slice of tenth-century Viking life. The last phase of the row of wooden houses is preserved as it was found by

Jorvik

The thatched houses, which doubled as workshops, crowded on to Coppergate with their roofs almost touching. To the surprise of archaeologists, the boundaries of the properties fronting on to the street had not changed substantially in a thousand years – the twentieth-century shops followed the same alignments. The stalls along the street sold leather shoes with detachable uppers; 'junk' jewellery hastily cast in lead alloy and given a quick silvery finish; wooden bowls and plates (some were found half-finished in one of the houses); carved bone combs, woollen cloth and knitting needles.

Deep underground in the Jorvik Viking Centre, visitors to this museum glide through medieval Coppergate in silent electric cars; between the thatched houses, right through the inside of one house and along to the waterfront where a Viking trading vessel discharges furs from the Baltic, quern-stones and pottery from the Rhineland, wine from France and silks from the East.

In York the trading vessel would have taken on leather goods, textiles, wool and no doubt some of the bric-à-brac on sale in Coppergate. The archaeological finds fully support the view of the tenth-century traveller who described the town as being 'enriched with the treasure of merchants who come from all quarters, particularly the Danish people'.

But the smell of Viking York must have been awful, and the Jorvik Centre lets you have a whiff of it amongst the babble of Old Norse street cries and the seagull sound effects. The vigorous people who lived in Coppergate, beautifully modelled in the museum display and wearing clothes copied from examples dug out of the excavated houses, heaved so much rubbish into their back yards and streets that the ground level rose during the tenth century by about 2 centimetres a year. Rubbish pits, latrines and wells that were dug too close to each other ensured that Jorvik's population was less than healthy. The contents of the latrines, for example, carefully sieved by archaeologists, showed that everyone had worms. They died like flies in

Top: *Coppergate, a reconstructed street in Viking York. At the end of the the row of thatched houses, a Viking boat (centre top of picture) discharges its cargo.*

Above: *Excavated house timbers conserved and displayed where they were found about 6 metres below street level, under the Jorvik Centre. Made of oak, some walls survived to a height of 1.8 metres in rooms with an average size of 7 by 3 metres.*

childhood; over half of all women died before the age of thirty-five and anyone who reached the age of sixty was very lucky.

the York Archaeological Trust in the basement of the new Coppergate shopping complex.

Alfred the Great

Not only York, but the entire country, was well on the way to falling into the orbit of the Scandinavian world by the time that Alfred the Great succeeded his brother as king of the south-western English kingdom of Wessex in 871. At that time, Wessex itself was under attack, East Anglia and Northumbria had fallen and Mercia, a kingdom in what is now the English Midlands, was to succumb in 874. If Wessex fell, the Viking King Guthrum would complete his victory in this ninth-century Battle of Britain.

In Hampshire, Wiltshire and Dorset (all parts of Wessex) the *Anglo-Saxon Chronicle* reported battles lost and won, and by 878 the campaign was going so badly that Alfred had been reduced to waging guerrilla warfare from a base hidden in the Somerset marshes. 'He had nothing to live on except what he could forage by frequent raids,' Alfred's biographer, Bishop Asser, re-

called. In later editions of Asser's book another writer has added anecdotes which tell of Alfred trying his hand as a pastry cook and penetrating the Viking lines disguised as a minstrel.

What is not clear from any source is how the king was able to turn this military disaster around. Asser and the *Anglo-Saxon Chronicle* skip the details and leave us to imagine 'one mighty leap' that took Alfred from the wilderness up to the head of a successful English force. He fell upon the Vikings at Edington in Wiltshire where 'he destroyed the Viking army with great slaughter, and pursued those who fled as far as the stronghold, hacking them down'. Even more remarkable were the terms of the truce between Alfred and the Viking King Guthrum who agreed to 'accept Christianity and to receive baptism at King Alfred's hand'. Nonetheless, most of eastern England and the north remained in Viking hands and became known as the 'Danelaw', where Danish settlers, speaking a language not dissimilar to Old English, lived according to their own law and traditions. Alfred, who by this

Right: *A page of Alfred's 'Pastoral Rule', now in the Bodleian Library, Oxford.*

The Alfred Jewel, perhaps the ornate top of a book mark, was found in Devon in the seventeenth century. Inscribed on its edge in Latin is 'Alfred ordered me to be made'.

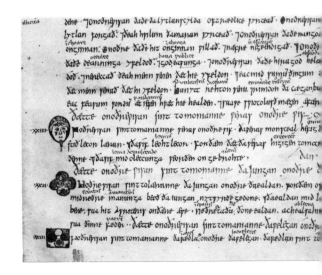

Danish settlements in England ('Danelaw')

Late-ninth-century boundary agreed by King Alfred and the Danish King Guthrum

• Alfred's burhs

Warwick

Worcester

Buckingham

Cricklade

Malmesbury

Oxford

Wallingford

Sashes

Bath

Southwark

Watchet

Axbridge

Chisbury

Pilton

Lyng

Langport

Eashing

Shaftesbury

Winchester

Eorpeburnan

Exeter

Bridport

Southampton

Portchester

Lewes

Lydford

Wareham

Chichester

Hastings

Halwell

Christchurch

there were at least thirty-three burhs, including three in Mercia. In what must have been a flurry of efficient organisation, most of them were completed in ten to twelve years.

Alfred's burhs were tested in 892 when another great army from Denmark, reinforced by settlers from the Danelaw, tried to break into Wessex. The burhs turned them back and, in the peaceful years that followed, Alfred was able to concentrate on updating English laws and pursue the cause of English learning. The use of Latin had declined so much during the years of war that, according to Asser, Alfred ordered his judges to learn it or leave office. And then that remarkable and far-sighted warrior king decided to learn Latin himself. His purpose? To translate into English 'some of the books that may be necessary for all men to know'.

He surrounded himself with men of letters, just as Charlemagne had done a century before, but Alfred translated several works himself including a manual for bishops. Bede's enduring work *The History of the English Church and People* was translated from Latin under Alfred's patronage. In these works we see the beginning of

time had established himself as a national leader, took the western part of Mercia and all of Wessex, which later also included the old kingdom of Kent.

Alfred had negotiated the breathing space he needed before the next – and inevitable – Viking onslaught. While the Danes were starting to farm their conquered lands, to adopt Christianity and to intermarry with the Anglo-Saxons, Alfred was formulating a plan for the future defence of Wessex. It was based on the Burhs, or Boroughs. These were towns that Alfred either created or adapted as fortified settlements in strategic positions. His aim was to block any Viking advance into his kingdom. No burh was more than 32 kilometres, or a day's march, from the next. In all

Wareham

Wareham's earthen ramparts are massive enough to be mistaken for natural features of the landscape. There is, however, no doubt about their ninth-century origins and, although a precise date is difficult to arrive at, they are a tangible connection with Alfred's time. Building the 20-metre-wide and 6-metre-high ramparts was a colossal task in itself, and the provision of manpower according to the system devised by Alfred proved to be equally monumental. The young king overcame the perennial problem of keeping early medieval armies together – soldiers tended to drift away to their land – by splitting the army into two parts: one to be on duty, while the other continued to farm. An Anglo-Saxon document called the *Burghal Hidage*, the earliest surviving English civil service 'file', records how many men were needed for the defence of Wessex.

The manpower levy was based on land. Every hide of agricultural land (about 16–20 hectares in Wessex) had to provide one man for the defence of his local burh, and each pole (5 metres) of wall was allocated four men. On that basis historians have estimated that the thirty burhs within the ancient boundaries of Wessex would have needed 27 000 men. The Burh of Wareham was assessed at 1600 hides, which implied that the walls were more than 2 kilometres in circumference.

With Jonathan Riley-Smith I scrambled up Wareham's steep ramparts – some 6 metres above street level – that would have offered a magnificent view in case of attack.

Wareham's Alfredian defences still embrace the modern town on three sides. Two Anglo-Saxon churches survive and, from the footpath on top of the ramparts, you can see how the streets conform to a neat grid pattern laid down by Anglo-Saxon town planners. It looks as if the burhs were conceived not just as fortresses, but as part of a large-scale plan of urban expansion. Settlers were attracted to the plots of land and houses within the safety of the ramparts and, in time, the burhs, with their own courts and mints, became important commercial centres. One of the most remarkable achievements of Anglo-Saxon royal government was a standardised coinage for the whole kingdom – five million coins in circulation at any one time, struck from dies supplied to the burhs by royal officials.

Wareham, Dorset, one of Alfred's burhs, which still retains its massive defensive ramparts on three sides of the town. The Anglo-Saxon street grid plan can be seen clearly.

English prose. English had been used before in books of law and in heroic poetry, but Alfred demonstrated that English had a far wider application and that it could also be a powerful language of learning.

When Alfred became king in 871 on the death of his brother Athelred, the succession had been decided by a small group of nobles who chose Alfred ahead of the king's own sons. There were no clear rules governing succession, and decisions, sometimes made on the battlefield, had to be taken quickly. But in most cases royal blood was a prerequisite. This concept of English kingship was deeply rooted in pagan history and ancestry. Alfred claimed descent from Woden, but his biographer added Noah and Adam for good measure.

Anglo-Saxon Royal Government

In Christian times kings were anointed with holy oil by a bishop during the coronation ceremony. This was believed to imbue them with the power to intercede with God. They were expected to protect their subjects from natural disasters such as crop failure and pestilence, and in that act of anointing we see the emergence of 'the divine right of kings', a concept which was to endure through to the seventeenth century. But the first time we hear of an anointed king in England is during Charlemagne's reign when the idea appears to have crossed the North Sea in time for the crowning of Offa's son Eogrith in 787; even today the coronation ceremony retains many elements that would be familiar to a late Anglo-Saxon king.

Church and state in Anglo-Saxon England worked closely together. Bishops, for example, were among the king's advisers. The clerics who ran the royal chapel probably doubled as the king's administrators, but the kingdom had no permanent capital. The kings took their entourage around the country, staying in the palaces they maintained, where they held Witans, or policy-making assemblies. More than seven Anglo-Saxon palaces have been identified in recent years, including the early seventh-century Northumbrian palace at Yeavering. Excavated in the late 1950s and early 1960s, it showed up as a complex of large timber assembly halls and out-buildings. One surprising feature identified by its post holes was a stadium for public meetings that was probably not unlike a Roman amphitheatre.

The palace we visited at Cheddar in Somerset was started in Alfred's time, and was said to have been one of his favourites. It is similar in style to Yeavering, but there is no sign of a stadium. A charter, however, does survive from a Witan that was held there in 968, during Edgar's reign, which tells us much about the nature of the assembly – how the king in the Great Hall presided over delegates who included the Archbishop of Canterbury and earls who represented royal government in the shires.

Government of the shires was through county courts where writs despatched by the king were read. The system, which was borrowed from Charlemagne's empire, reached its apogee in the middle of the tenth century when the shires were subdivided into 'hundreds' with their own courts that dealt with theft and violence in the area. In fact, the Anglo-Saxons left an indelible mark on English county life. Anglo-Saxon shire boundaries were hardly changed until the re-organisation of local government in 1974.

In Anglo-Saxon England, if a noble failed to turn up at a Witan the king might take it as a sign of rebellion and move against him, so the most powerful men in the kingdom left their lands in the shires to attend the king for weeks on end. In

Cheddar Palace

Cheddar Palace must have looked something like this when Witans were held there in Edgar's reign between 959 and 975. With the royal forest of Mendip and the spectacular Cheddar Gorge nearby, it was a popular place for meeting. In Alfred's time it was said to have been one of his favourite palaces.

Horsemen returning from a hunt (top centre) pass the flagpole from which would have flown the royal standard of Wessex – a golden dragon on a red or purple background. Ahead of them (centre) is the Great Hall, about 25 metres long and 6 metres wide, made of plank walls with shuttered windows and a shingle roof. The kitchen was identified to the right of the hall. The excavation of 1960–2 also revealed the post holes of outhouses, such as the latrine block near the door of the Great

Hall. The only stone building found was the chapel (centre left). The remaining buildings were the 'bower', or women's quarters (far left centre), and in the foreground a grain store, mill and bakery. Alan Sorrell's drawing (below) is based on how the palace might have looked in the second of its six phases of construction and occupation between 930 and 1000.

As with all known Anglo-Saxon timber buildings there is very little to see today. If a new school had not been planned for the site we might never have located the shadowy evidence of the posts that supported these buildings, and all that remains is a confusing array of concrete stumps in front of the appropriately named Kings of Wessex School. The only upstanding building that echoes Cheddar's royal past is a small thirteenth-century ruined chapel in which the excavators found a mould for casting a church bell.

the Witan we see one of the most important factors in English history at work – geography. England, unlike many of the kingdoms of continental Europe, was compact enough for such *national* assemblies to be held, and in Edgar's reign his royal administration was considered to be the most efficient in Western Europe.

Edgar's reign from 959 to 975 accounted for the golden years of the Anglo-Saxon kingdom. Edgar was head of the oldest royal house in Europe; he was connected by marriage to many of the important ruling families of continental Europe; his scholars and clerics in the great English Christian centres such as Winchester and Canterbury were closely in touch with their counterparts in abbeys such as Cluny, and during Edgar's reign English monasteries were reformed. Literature and art flourished, and a strong navy kept the Vikings at bay. Edgar was also the monarch who could demand recognition from most parts of Britain, and one chronicler underlines the extent of the king's power with a description of him in his royal barge being rowed along the River Dee by a group of British and Irish kings who had done him homage. Edgar died in 975 on the eve of another prolonged Danish offensive – one that was to inflict untold misery on England for more than forty years.

Aethelred the Unready, Edgar's unfortunate son, had to face the renewed onslaught. His nickname is better translated as 'the uncounselled' – it is a pun on Aethelred which means 'good counsel' – but, badly advised or not, the kingdom was hardly ready for the persistent fury of the Viking attacks. Aethelred's reputation has come down to us, perhaps a little unfairly, as an incompetent and treacherous monarch. He was,

however, competent enough to stay the course of a particularly long reign of thirty-seven years, but the *Anglo-Saxon Chronicle* attributes the beginning of the onerous 'Danegeld' tax to him.

English gold and silver poured out of the kingdom's estimated seventy mints as Aethelred tried to use England's wealth to buy peace. The renewed Viking attacks that began in 980 were no less destructive than the armies Alfred had fought. Every few years, harassment along the coast was augmented by large Viking armies marching across the shires, and with every incursion the 'Danegeld', the price of peace, went up.

Taxes levied by the efficient Anglo-Saxon administration ended up in Scandinavia, where large hoards of coin have been uncovered by archaeologists. At least 50 000 English silver pennies, minted between 980 and 1050, have been found. All of them came from concealed hoards, which suggests that we are looking only at a fraction of the loot that crossed the North Sea.

Aethelred retaliated by ordering the massacre of peaceful Danish settlers on St Brice's Day, 13 November 1002. Many died in the act of political paranoia, and that same year, in a bid to make a closer alliance with the Duchy of Normandy, Aethelred married Duke Richard's daughter, Emma. However, Viking pressure continued from bases in Denmark, the Isle of Man, the Scottish islands and Ireland. The campaign of the Danish king Sweyn (Forkbeard) and his son Canute, ended with what amounted to a Viking victory, Canute the young prince dividing England between himself and Aethelred's son, Edmund Ironside. Edmund died almost before the scribes had finished copying the treaty and the English establishment, by now weary of war, offered the crown of the whole of England to the Viking prince, Canute.

In this way, England was completely drawn into a Scandinavian empire that included Denmark, Norway and part of Sweden. And the influence of the long Viking rule still shows through in modern English; Scandinavian words such as take, call, window, husband, sky, anger, scant and happy are but a few examples of very many loan words. Many place names in the north and east of England also display their Scandinavian roots. Villages and towns and cities whose names end in '-thorpe' or '-by' have the Danes to thank. The word law itself is Danish and the origins of the English jury system almost certainly lie in Danelaw.

The Anglo-Saxon princes who survived went into exile, including the future king, Edward the Confessor. He went to Normandy, his mother's birthplace. The other young princes went to Hungary. Canute, in what must have been a bid for the hearts and minds of Englishmen, brought Aethelred's widow, Emma, back from exile in Normandy and married her. He thenceforth behaved like a devout Christian, ruled with English advisers and gave the country almost twenty years of peace, but he exacted a heavy price. The abhorred Danegeld tax continued to be collected through the well-established system of royal government.

Canute himself spent most of his time in Denmark. He ruled England through earls, who built up enormous power. Earl Godwine of Wessex, for example, was one of Canute's four vice-regents in England, and Godwine's son, Harold Godwine, was destined to become King of England. Earl Odda was another powerful man. Towards the end of his career, he was responsible for Gloucestershire and Worcestershire. It was on his estate at Deerhurst in Gloucestershire that Canute and Edmund Ironside are said to have drawn up their treaty of partition. Today, only a small chapel remains as evidence of Odda's power and prestige.

With the marriage of Canute to Aethelred's Norman-born widow Emma, the Anglo-Saxon monarchy began its tortuous path towards the Norman invasion of 1066. Canute had a son by Emma called Harthacnut and by his other wife, Aelfgifu, two more sons called Swein and Harold.

When Canute died in 1035, Harthacnut, his chosen successor, was ruling Denmark on behalf of his father and was bogged down with political troubles. He did not come to England, so his mother summoned his half-brother, Alfred (Aethelred's second son), from exile in Normandy. But Alfred was murdered by Harold's supporters in connivance, it is thought, with Earl Godwine. Harold I, Canute's son by Aelfgifu, became king but he died after only five years and very little about his reign has been discovered.

The next choice of a king, a compromise between the rival parties grouped around Canute's former queens, brought Harthacnut back from Denmark and his surviving half-brother, Edward (Emma and Aethelred's third son), from Normandy. Harthacnut was crowned and the French-speaking Edward was given some role of 'association' in the kingship. In under two years Harthacnut died and in 1042 another decision was taken that pointed the kingdom towards Normandy and catastrophe for Anglo-Saxon England. The throne was offered to Edward – unmarried, celibate, pious, but with the blood of Cerdic and Alfred running in his veins.

During Edward's long reign the earls of Wessex increased their already considerable

Odda's Chapel

Odda's Chapel is one of England's Anglo-Saxon buildings that went missing for a few centuries. It was rediscovered in 1885, masquerading as a half-timbered medieval farmhouse. A clergyman noticed Anglo-Saxon windows behind some plaster during alterations to the building, but it was not until 1965 that the farmhouse and historical buildings were separated to allow visitors to step into a fragment of Odda's world. For Jonathan Riley-Smith and myself, it was a rare chance to explore a building of the eleventh century which remains virtually unchanged to this day.

A medieval stone window head dated the chapel. It turned out to be a slab from an altar bearing the inscription 'In honour of the Holy Trinity this altar has been dedicated.' And those words tie up neatly with another inscription, found near the building in the seventeenth century, which reads, 'Earl Odda had this royal hall built and dedicated in honour of the Holy Trinity for the soul of his brother Aelfric which left the body in this place. Bishop Ealdred dedicated it the Second of the Ides of April in the fourteenth year of the reign of King Edward of the English.' The date of the chapel is therefore fixed: 12 April 1056 – a rare piece of dating for any Anglo-Saxon building.

When Odda completed his memorial chapel it was part of a complex of monastic buildings which had been given to him by Edward the Confessor. Odda's name appears on many of the charters issued by Edward after he became king in 1042. When Earl Godwine was exiled in 1051, Odda was made earl over Somerset, Devon, Dorset and Cornwall, but Godwine and his sons soon regained favour and Odda ended up with the scattered estates that included the abbey of Deerhurst. The earl would also have been responsible for the supply of men for the army. In times of stress he would have called out the select 'fyrd' – one conscript for every hide of land – and on rare occasions such as the invasion of William the Conqueror, all able-bodied men would answer the call of the 'great fyrd'.

Odda's Chapel, with its Romanesque arch between the chancel and the nave, has a replica of the Odda Stone above the place where the altar once stood (the original inscription is in the Ashmolean Museum, Oxford) and it is clear that no major structural changes have been made over the years to spoil the original building. Odda himself became a monk at Deerhurst but never lived to see the completed chapel. When he died, on 31 August 1053, he was mourned as a lover of churches, the friend of the poor and oppressed, and a guardian of virginity.

Earl Odda's Chapel, dated to 1056. For centuries it had been 'lost' within a Gloucestershire farmhouse. The stone wing at the end of the house (left) was identified as Odda's Chapel in 1885.

power built up during Canute's long absence from England. By the 1060s Harold, Earl of Wessex, Earl Godwine's son, was to all intents and purposes running the kingdom. He had even married off his sister to the celibate king and, as Edward lay dying in January 1066, Harold saw himself as the natural successor. Moreover, he claimed that Edward had offered him the succession on his deathbed. He was backed in this view by another onlooker, Archbishop Stigand. Edward the Confessor died on 5 January 1066 and the next day, in Edward's newly completed Westminster Abbey, Harold was crowned King Harold II of England.

The Norman Invasion

News of Harold's crowning did not go down well in Normandy. Duke William, fifth of his line since the Viking Rollo had founded the duchy at the beginning of the tenth century, believed that Edward had promised him the throne, and he vowed to take it. William's character was like hardened steel, and it was further toughened by the stigma of his illegitimate birth. His father, Duke Robert, had scooped up the pretty young daughter of a tanner when he was out riding one day and carried her off. William was the product of this passionate union, and the title of bastard dogged his career. A seasoned warrior, William was ruler of a very successful and militaristic state which had exported its martial strength as far as southern Italy where, by 1066, the Normans were poised to add the island of Sicily to their Italian empire.

Norman expansion was in the air and William was determined to make England the next Norman prize. He sought Papal approval for the invasion, and got it. Next he set about building hundreds of ships for the short, but often dangerous, crossing to the English coast.

During the winter and spring of 1066, in the lead-up to William's invasion, a second contender was preparing to do battle for the English throne. He was the Norwegian King Harald Hardrada ('hard counsel') who had ruled Norway for twenty years after the break-up of Canute's Scandinavian empire. Harold Godwinson, the English king, had no way of knowing when the Norwegian Harald would strike, but just across the English Channel William's preparations were obvious.

Harold Godwinson called out the Great Fyrd on the south coast of England and positioned his fleet at Sandwich and the Isle of Wight, where the ships waited for weeks during the summer. Nothing happened. The weather was against William and, perhaps believing that the invasion had been postponed, Harold stood the fyrd down and the fleet sailed round to London.

The wind, however, was just right for the Norwegian Harald, who crossed the North Sea with an army of about 9000 men. York, the former capital of the last Viking king, Eric Bloodaxe, was overrun by Harald Hardrada's troops on 20 September 1066. Harold Godwinson gathered his army, marched north in four days, and surprised the Norwegians at Stamford Bridge just outside York early on the morning of 25 September. The element of surprise was such that the English forces scored a complete victory over the Norwegians and their English ally, Tostig, Harold Godwinson's disaffected brother. England had been spared another Viking conquest.

Almost before the cries of victory had been stilled Harold Godwinson heard that William of Normandy had landed unopposed at Pevensey on 28 September. It meant that Harold then had to march half the length of England, with a battle-weary army, to confront the new threat. Pausing in London to collect reinforcements, perhaps some of the Danish mercenaries he had sent for at the beginning of the year, he arrived at the escarpment on the edge of the downs, six miles north-west of Hastings, where the little Sussex town of Battle stands today, on the evening of 13 October.

Battle of Hastings

William's scouts must have reported the news that the English army was approaching. In response, the Norman columns moved up from the coast to meet Harold. There would be no advantage of surprise in this battle. William's troops assembled on low ground less than a quarter of a mile from Harold, across uneven and marshy ground. Harold's forces already occupied a commanding position along the top of a ridge overlooking the battlefield.

Before the battle, William, who had hung the sacred relics from Bayeux around his neck, attended a mass said by two bishops who were accompanying the army. He also gave the troops a pep talk: 'If you bear yourselves valiantly, you will obtain victory, honour and riches. If not, you will be ruthlessly butchered or led ignominiously as captives into the hands of pitiless enemies.' William of Poitiers, who recorded William's words, also tells us that Duke William consoled the nervous troops with the thought that the English had never been able to resist invaders and that they 'had not ever been famed as soldiers'.

The stragglers in Harold's army were still arriving as 'the terrible sound of trumpets on both sides signalled the beginning of the battle'. One of the English records of the battle, that of Florence of Worcester, says that only one third of Harold's forces were in position at the start of the engagement. But Harold's well-trained house-carls, his élite troops, occupied the high ground

and the Norman knights would have had a difficult job advancing uphill and breaking this well-disciplined line of defence.

The whole story of the Norman invasion, seen from the Norman point of view, is laid out in the beautiful Bayeux Tapestry which was commissioned soon after the invasion. The history of this 70-metre long and 40-centimetre high tapestry is fascinating. As far as we know this work was put in hand by Duke William's half-brother, Bishop Odo of Bayeux, as a decoration for his newly built cathedral. The shape of the marks on the back of the tapestry could have come from being tied to the pillars of a large building, which tends to support that story. The great work, which survived a series of devastating medieval fires, was left on a roll and occasionally pulled out and shown to visitors. But it was almost lost in 1792 when Napoleon's troops took over the town, found the tapestry and wanted to cut it up to use as wagon covers. Wiser counsels prevailed and the tapestry survived, and it is now beautifully displayed in what was once the palace of the Bishop of Bayeux. The tapestry depicts Harold doing homage to William (becoming William's liege man) on a visit to Normandy two or three years before Edward died. The written sources, except the scanty English accounts, seem to support the story on the tapestry, and some modern historians believe that William may also have visited Edward in England.

Scene by scene the tapestry gives its version of events: the politics of Harold's oath-taking; the foresters felling trees to build the invasion fleet; the embarkation of the knights and their horses, the landing on the south coast of England; and all the gory details of the battle of Hastings.

Bayeux

Right: *Harold Godwinson swearing an oath to William in Bayeux Cathedral. Harold has his hands on two holy reliquaries: the bones of two of Normandy's saints; and a bottle containing a drop of Christ's blood. In medieval eyes, an oath sworn on relics was a deeply solemn event.*

The invasion fleet probably amounted to about 400 boats and 8000–10 000 men with all their horses and equipment. The horses pictured here seem to be enjoying the sea breeze. It has been estimated that about 2000 knights were included in the force. The rich pickings at stake had attracted knights from many different states: France, Flanders, Anjou, Brittany (settled centuries earlier by Romano-British fleeing from the Saxon invasion of England) and Spain; and some Normans had travelled from Italy to join Duke William's widely advertised invasion.

The English, who had no cavalry, were armed with big battleaxes and swords, and grouped themselves behind a wall of interlocking shields that made an effective barrier, even against the mounted knights.

The Norman army was mainly composed of archers, heavily armed infantry and cavalry. The archers advanced and rained arrows down on the English. The infantry followed, and (right) the cavalry armed with swords or javelins were put in last to take advantage of any weakness in the English lines.

The battle ended when King Harold was killed after a lucky hit by a Norman archer. Harold is seen here with an arrow in his eye, and in the next scene he is cut down by a knight.

The battle began at 9 a.m. Norman archers, followed by heavily armed infantry, advanced across the difficult terrain. But as William of Poitiers tells us, 'The English resisted valiantly, each man according to his strength, and they hurled back spears and javelins and weapons of all kinds together with axes and stones fastened to pieces of wood.' The Normans fell back in disarray, and the sight of the enemy fleeing was too much of a temptation for the soldiers on Harold's flank. They gave chase. To save a deteriorating situation, William took off his helmet so that all his troops could see that he was still in command, gave a rousing speech and counter-attacked with his cavalry. The knights pursued the English foot soldiers 'and cut them down so that not one escaped'.

The cavalry then tried to breach the enemy lines by galloping as best they could up the hill to where the row of shields still held firm. But, again, the Norman advance failed. William, having seen the weakness created when the English broke ranks to chase retreating infantry, tried a 'feint' retreat. He ordered his cavalry to attack and retreat, apparently in confusion. On a signal, the knights wheeled around in a well-rehearsed manoeuvre and cut down their pursuers. Twice the trick worked and 'several thousand' English were slaughtered.

Harold had no time to restore order. The sky rained arrows shot high into the air to fall on the English forces behind the front line. As the tapestry shows, one arrow hit Harold in the eye. We stood on the spot, marked by the altar of a later abbey church, where the king is reputed to have fallen. English confidence flagged and further cavalry charges broke through the long line of shields. Harold, still wielding an axe, was cut down by a Norman knight. Demoralised, the English began to scatter, and the battle was lost.

Battle Abbey

The small town of Battle in Sussex takes its name from Battle Abbey, now at the end of the high street, which was so named because of the most famous battle in English history. The abbey, which still dominates the town, was founded by William the Conqueror to mark the spot where Harold fell with an arrow in his eye, and the abbey church was built so that the altar was directly over that spot. Today it is marked by an inscribed slab put there

Ruins of the thirteenth-century east range of Battle Abbey. William the Conqueror built the original Abbey, parts of which still survive on the site of the Battle of Hastings.

'The blood-stained battleground was covered with the flower of youth and nobility of England', and the road to London was open to William the Conqueror.

Duke William of Normandy and his jubilant army were the victors of the battlefield, but an entire country had yet to be subdued. William called for reinforcements from Normandy and marched north towards London having given his men a few days' rest. Romney, Dover, Canterbury and Winchester all submitted to William as

after the footings of the church had been revealed by archaeologists. Some of the eleventh-century building also survives above ground, and in the east range you can walk through well-preserved thirteenth-century ground-floor rooms with lofty vaulted ceilings.

Walking a few yards south of the altar of the church brings you to the brow of the hill overlooking the battlefield. Jonathan and I found that it is still unspoiled open country. Wearing stout shoes we walked the battlefield, starting at an orientation centre which English Heritage has set up near the splendid fourteenth-century abbey gatehouse. The footpath took us along to a gorse-covered hillock from where William would have viewed the English lines. The marshy ground, combined with the steep slope up to the abbey, makes you realise the difficulties that William faced.

The best surviving of the abbey's medieval buildings is the gatehouse – almost a castle in itself. It is certainly impressive with its crenellated towers, ornate carving and separate entrances for pedestrians and vehicles. Today, though, it is the entrance to a school which occupies the sixteenth-century mansion built after the dissolution of the monasteries.

Battle Abbey gatehouse. Built in 1338 it survived Henry VIII's destruction of the monasteries to serve as a manorial courthouse.

he followed a circuitous route towards his goal.

Failing to force his way across London Bridge from the Southwark bank, the conqueror marched through Surrey, Hampshire, crossed the Thames at Wallingford and pitched camp at Berkhamsted. Thus he almost circumnavigated London and effectively cut off Saxon communications and support from the north of England. At Berkhamsted the campaign to subdue Anglo-Saxon England ended. The surviving English nobles led by Edgar Atheling went to William's tent and offered him the crown; and, on Christmas Day at Westminster Abbey, William Duke of Normandy was crowned King of England. Once again, a foreign ruler had taken control of the Anglo-Saxon kingdom; however, this monarch, unlike his Scandinavian predecessors, had no intention of being absorbed by the well-established civilisation he had conquered.

CHAPTER THREE

French-Speaking Foreigners

*T*he ecclesiastical and military complex that so confidently sits astride Durham still gives the impression of unyielding power. Jonathan and I could almost feel it as we approached the castle through Durham's narrow cobbled streets, which still have medieval timber-framed houses behind their Georgian façades. The cathedral and castle are on a rocky plateau that rises high above the city. It is almost an island site in a generous loop of the River Wear and, looking up from the river bank, the view has hardly changed since the Middle Ages.

It is a reminder that the initial impact the Normans had on the English was not on their character. It was on the landscape that the Normans first made their presence and power felt. Castles sprouted everywhere once they arrived. In the beginning, they were modest affairs – just a 'keep' made out of timber and placed on top of a large mound of earth (a motte). A deep ditch protected the mound and extended around the earthen rampart that enclosed the 'bailey' – the castle courtyard. The motte and bailey castles were effective. Like Roman marching forts, they could be erected quickly during a military campaign.

William's first castle was built within the walls of the Roman shore fort at Pevensey. Another motte and bailey castle sprang up at Hastings, probably constructed from prefabricated components brought across from Normandy. However, these two castles were never translated into permanent stone buildings like the one to be found in the corner of Portchester's Roman fort

or the Tower of London. Every move the Normans made in England was followed by a castle. 'The fortifications called castles by the Normans were scarcely known in the English provinces, and so the English, in spite of their love of fighting, could put up only a weak resistance to their enemies.' The chronicler, Orderic Vitalis, gives the impression of a network of castles by the mid-1070s. The Domesday survey of 1086 mentions at least fifty, and by the early twelfth century every community of any size was dominated by a castle plonked down on a prime site with little or no regard for what had been there before. It is easy to imagine the effect on Anglo-Saxon morale as houses were swept away and streets diverted after the arrival of the Normans.

Castles and cavalry, however, were not able to keep the lid on English resentment. Rebellion boiled over in the south-west, in the Midlands and in the north of England. In every case William's knights stamped out the resistance with ruthless efficiency. Huge swathes of countryside were laid waste by burning crops and villages. The population either scattered or was killed and, if Domesday is right, even seventeen years later some northern counties 'harried' by William had not recovered.

The Danes, still watching for a chance to reclaim Canute's lost kingdom, complicated matters by allying themselves with the English resistance. A large Danish army, fighting alongside the English pretender to the throne, Edgar the Atheling (King Aethelred's great-grandson), was defeated by the Normans at York in 1069. Danish warriors also fought together with Hereward the Wake to defend his Isle of Ely base in the fens of East Anglia. But by 1081 resistance in England had largely petered out and the Danish invasion plan of 1085 – which never materialised – was the epilogue to almost four centuries of intermittent invasion, settlement and rule by Scandinavians.

England was now under new management. The knights and nobles who had fought with William were rewarded with English land, and by 1086 only about six out of 180 major land-owners were Anglo-Saxon. The landed nobles were now foreign and French-speaking almost to a man. The top jobs in the Church and the monasteries were also handed out to Normans. The twelfth-century chronicler, William of Malmesbury, remarked, 'England had become a residence for foreigners and the property of aliens. There is no English Earl, no Bishop nor Abbot; strangers all, they prey upon the riches and the vitals of England.'

A subtle but major change that the 'strangers' wrought on England was an unusual land-holding system with William the Conqueror as landlord of England and everyone else as his tenant. The tenants-in-chief, Norman barons and the few English earls who had managed to hang on to their lands, paid rent assessed in numbers of mail-clad knights. The bigger the estate, the larger the number of knights who had to be available to fight for the king. The barons sublet, again for 'knight service', to lesser nobles, who in turn might grant more 'fiefs' in a complicated pyramid of landholding with the king always at the top. At the bottom of the heap the Anglo-Saxon peasantry lost out badly. The number of slaves may have been reduced after the Conquest, but an increasing number of free peasants became feudal serfs. They and their families could be bought and sold by their Norman lords like goods and chattels. But everyone, including the nobles, was liable to severe punishment if they trespassed on the vast tracts of forests all over England that William reserved for hunting.

The Domesday Survey

William's remarkable survey of the kingdom in 1086 confirms the redistribution of wealth in England. Called 'Domesday' because its parchment pages virtually contained the last judge-

Norman and Plantagenet Dominions in Western Europe.

ment in any land dispute, William's initiative was not popular with the Anglo-Saxon chronicler. 'So very thoroughly did he have the inquiry carried out that there was not a single hide, not one virgate of land even – it is shameful to record it, but it did not seem shameful for him to do it – not even one ox, nor one cow, nor one pig, which escaped notice in the survey. And all the surveys were subsequently brought to him.'

Page after page of the survey tells of land that had changed hands after the Norman invasion: '. . . in the hundred of Uttlesford William Cardon appointed 1 freeman with 8 acres. He belongs to (Great) Chishill, of Geoffrey de Mandeville's holding. Value – 2 shillings . . .' And in the hundred of Dunmow in Essex: '. . . In "Plesingho" a freeman held 1 hide of land, which Humphrey Golden Bollocks annexed . . . 7 small holders, 2 slaves, woodland, 30 pigs, meadow, 7 acres; then (at the time of the conquest) 1 mill. Value then 16 shillings; now 23 shillings.'

The purpose of Domesday is still a matter of argument among historians; was it simply a rapacious way to tighten the tax screws on the population, or an attempt to clear up any ambiguities concerning the redistribution of land? It was certainly a remarkable feat of organisation on the part of Anglo-Saxon 'civil servants' in the lower levels of government. They must have been able to draw on extensive local records to put the survey together in such a short time. Sadly, those records have not survived, probably because they would have been of little use to French-speaking Norman clerks who were later in charge. It is argued by Professor W. L. Warren that the much-vaunted Norman efficiency became nothing less than 'ramshackle' about fifty years after the 'Domesday generation' of Anglo-Saxon administrators died out; 'the Normans did not wish to preserve the Anglo-Saxon inheritance nor did they know how to'.

But the first two or three generations of Normans did know how to build. England was rich and the newcomers poured their newly acquired wealth into a building boom that, in William of Malmesbury's view, transformed the country. 'After their coming to England, you might see churches in every village, and in the towns and cities monasteries built after a style unknown before; you could watch the country flourishing.' William the Conqueror's Norman bishops embarked on a building programme that virtually replaced all Anglo-Saxon cathedrals in under forty years. In their place were built superb 'Romanesque' buildings which featured rounded windows, barrel-vaulted ceilings, solid cylindrical pillars and extravagantly decorated curved doorways. It was all on a massive scale and very impressive.

Although the Normans only ever accounted for about ten per cent of the population, it is perhaps not surprising that the Anglo-Saxons became so docile. The Normans considered everything about them to be inferior – even the Anglo-Saxons' saints. The learned and much respected Archbishop of Canterbury, Lanfranc, set the tone. 'These Englishmen among whom we are living have set up for themselves certain saints whom they revere. But sometimes when I turn over in my mind their own accounts of who they were, I cannot help having doubts about their sanctity.' Sceptical Norman clergy went about 'testing' the relics of English saints by throwing the centuries-old bones on the fire. If they did not burn up, the relics were considered to be genuine. In what must have been a profoundly shocking and sacrilegious act to the religious Anglo-Saxons, even the remains of the great St Cuthbert of Lindisfarne, whose shrine

Saint Cuthbert – a twelfth-century wall painting in the Galilee Chapel of Durham Cathedral.

was at Durham, were tested. His body had been in the Anglo-Saxon cathedral for almost a century before the Normans opened his oak coffin. It is said that inside they found the saint's body incorrupt, in perfect condition. Cuthbert's remains were allowed to rest in peace, and are still in Durham Cathedral which, more than any other, exemplifies the power with which the Normans ruled England.

When William the Conqueror died in 1087, the political drive that had held England and Normandy together abruptly broke. The fact was that William, like many strong rulers before him, had bungled the succession to his 'empire'. He had divided it between two of his sons: Rufus was given the English throne and Robert, who had given his father nothing but trouble, and had even led a rebellion against him, became Duke of Normandy. In 1096 Duke Robert answered the Pope's call to the first Crusade and, with a loan of 10 000 marks from Rufus, set off to capture Jerusalem. When he returned, victorious, to redeem his duchy, his brother Rufus, now King of England, was killed in what appeared to be a hunting accident. Immediately the Conqueror's youngest son, Henry, seized the throne. There ensued a bitter struggle between Robert and his brother Henry. It ended with Robert's capture and imprisonment for life.

Henry I's long reign, from 1100 to 1135, contributed much to the stability and well-being of England. He strengthened royal government and took the first steps towards founding the office of Chancellor of the Exchequer – named after the chequered boards used in accounting – and he made the king's courts more accessible and efficient. His marriage to Matilda, a niece of Edgar the Atheling, the last surviving member of the Anglo-Saxon royal family, was another positive move. It gave royal approval to intermarriage – a growing trend amongst the Norman nobility. To soften criticism and to strengthen his claim to lands, a Norman might try to marry into the Anglo-Saxon family who had been the original owners of the land in 1066.

Monasteries and the Church

In those difficult transitional times when the Normans still considered themselves the master race, one place where an Englishman could still make his mark was in a monastery. By the twelfth century there were hundreds of different monastic institutions, many of which tried to follow the basic sixth-century Benedictine rule of chastity, obedience and poverty. But although most monks had few personal possessions, monasteries became extremely rich from the exploitation of their huge land holdings.

They were like small towns in themselves. The monks employed large numbers of servants to

Durham

From almost anywhere in the city you can see the walls of Durham Castle with its round keep rising above them and, at the southern end of the rocky outcrop, the cathedral's grey towers. The second Norman Bishop of Durham, William of St Calais, started building the vast church in 1093, about twenty years after William had built the castle. Except for the tops of the towers and the Chapel of the Nine Altars, Durham is all eleventh- and twelfth-century work. It is simply the finest and most complete of all the Norman cathedrals in England.

The interior is just as impressive. It conveys a sense of power that makes you pause at the door before walking into the nave: enormously fat columns about 2 metres in diameter and almost

10 metres tall confront you. They are carved with designs of spirals, lozenges, fluting and chevrons, and lead your eye up past the Romanesque arches of the clerestory to the masterpiece of Durham – the roof. The Norman master mason had experimented with a new architectural style that would soon sweep across the whole of Western Europe: he had built the roof out of a series of vaults tied together by curved ribs of stone. The effect was dazzling. By distributing the weight of the stone through the ribs, the supporting piers and columns, the walls could be made thinner and the huge windows of the Gothic style made possible.

Without Cuthbert, the north of England's most popular saint from the Dark Ages, Durham might never have been built. St Cuthbert's remains, having passed the test of sanctity, clearly influenced the Normans' choice of site, and the new cathedral became an even bigger cult centre for the saint. His shrine, as described by a sixteenth-century Durham monk, was 'one of the most sumptuous monuments in all England, so great were the offerings and jewels bestowed on it, and endless miracles that were wrought on it, even in these later days'.

Henry VIII's commissioners put an end to all that when they broke up the shrine and confiscated its riches in 1537. But even then, when the coffin was opened, the body of the saint was reported as 'whole, incorrupt, with his face bare and his beard as if it had been a fortnight's growth, and his vestments upon him'. A list of items in the coffin is said to have included part of the rod of Moses, a piece of Jesus's manger, the claw of a griffin, ivory and crystal caskets, and cups and crosses set with precious jewels. The body of the saint was kept in the vestry until King Henry gave permission for it to be placed where it is today – under a plain marble slab on the spot where the medieval shrine once stood.

Durham is also the last resting place of the

Left: The cathedral, castle and monastery dominate the city of Durham today as they did in the twelfth century.

Venerable Bede, whose bones were stolen from Jarrow by an overzealous Durham monk in 1022. They were first added to Cuthbert's shrine, but in 1370 Bede was moved to the west end of the cathedral, where today his black stone tomb is not only an object of veneration but a tangible link with the 'father of English history'.

Jewelled cross from St Cuthbert's coffin, now in the cathedral's treasury. Parts of the coffin have also survived.

Below: *The interior of Durham Cathedral. In this Romanesque building the masons tried a new type of architecture – Gothic.*

cook, clean and carry; labourers were needed for the fields; other workmen for the upkeep of roads and bridges; and a management team of clerks to keep an eye on tenancy agreements and manorial courts. These clerks also collected the tithes that were due to the monastery from, perhaps, several parishes. The abbot or prior was in charge of a substantial corporation. Amongst his retainers he may have had a squadron of knights ready to serve the king as and when required, and his own public duties could have included sitting as a judge in the assize court or being on hand to advise the king.

Those priors and abbots who were English helped to keep English culture alive. Old Abbot Sampson of Bury St Edmunds, for example, enjoyed reading Anglo-Saxon literature in his spare time and, in church, preached in his Norfolk dialect. But the most important of all the monastic leaders was Abbot Ailred of Rievaulx, the son of a married English priest from Hexham in Northumberland. His order, the Cistercians, was founded at Cîteaux in Burgundy in 1098. One of its initiators was Stephen Harding, himself an Englishman. Its aim was to return to a purer form of Benedictine rule, and the Cistercians, who wore a habit made from undyed natural wool, were often called 'white monks'. To escape the distractions of medieval life, and to live their preferred life of self-denial, manual labour and self-sufficiency, they built their monasteries in remote and wild places. Their first monastery in England, at Waverley in Surrey, was built soon after they arrived in 1123. But it was at Ryedale in Yorkshire, where Rievaulx Abbey had been established in 1131, that Ailred first came across them.

Ailred had done well as a young man at the court of the Scottish King David and was destined for a high position in the Church.

Rievaulx Abbey

The ruins of Rievaulx Abbey combine enough upstanding buildings to evoke the heyday of a great medieval monastery with a dramatic and unspoiled rural setting. The strident calls of rooks or the flutter of pigeons high up among the buttresses and towers of the abbey ruins are sometimes the only sounds you might hear. Evocative of the Cistercian love of the wilderness? Not entirely. In Ailred's day the stone masons' chisels and the shouts of the workmen competing with the abbey bells must have been deafening at times. For years it was a vast building site and there was the problem of the neighbouring abbey of Byland. The monks at Byland, who were not Cistercians, had been given land less than a mile away – so close in fact that each community could hear the bells of the other day and night. Negotiations ended successfully with Byland's monks packing up and moving in 1145, the same year that Ailred took over Rievaulx as abbot. According to Ailred's biographer, Walter Daniel, the new abbot 'turned the house of Rievaulx into a stronghold for the sustaining of the weak . . . and so those wanderers of the world to whom no house of religion gave entrance, came to Rievaulx . . . and found the gates open'.

At its peak, about 650 monks lived in the monastery, but only a small proportion lived a cloistered existence. About 500 were lay brothers – taken on as glorified agricultural labourers who lived separately from the 140 professed monks. It was a scheme devised by the Cistercians so that the order could run its estates without letting the land to tenants and living off the rents like any other feudal landlord. Ailred's 'choir' monks could then devote themselves to the simple austere life of prayer and study that started every day at two in the morning when the bell summoned them.

There is enough of the monastery left to be able to follow the route the monks took throughout the day: the refectory walls stand to their full height; one corner of the arcade around the cloister has been reconstructed with slender pillars and carved capitals. The dormitory is not much more than a

is the nave (1140–5), which starts as a pure Romanesque building, but beyond the transepts the thirteenth-century east end is described by architectural historians as a masterpiece of Early English Gothic.

Ailred's influence in a predominantly Norman world extended beyond the architectural splendours of Ryedale. He was a prolific writer, and as well as religious and philosophical works, he wrote a biography of Edward the Confessor, and gave Rievaulx an important place in the intellectual life of England. At court, Ailred was an adviser to Henry II, the dynamic son of Geoffrey Plantagenet and Matilda, who added England to his Angevin empire in 1154. As abbot of a great monastery Ailred was also sought after as an adjudicator in ecclesiastical disputes all over the kingdom and that, combined with the need to inspect regularly Rievaulx's daughter houses, kept the abbot on the road for months at a time despite his increasingly poor health.

In his last year Ailred had a bed in the infirmary in front of the fire, where Walter Daniel described him as lying frail and twisted 'like a crumpled piece of parchment'. The walls of the infirmary at Rievaulx are still standing, some to their full height, and you can walk in there and see where the twelfth-century hearth must have been. There, Ailred lay on his pallet tormented by arthritic pain, hardly able to move. Over several days he called his monks, including Walter Daniel, to his bedside. 'For myself, I must confess that while I felt a great awe as I stood by his bed during those days, yet I also felt a joy greater than awe. For we heard him say continually: "Hasten, hasten", and he often urged his request with the name of Christ, which he spoke in English, because Christ's name in that tongue is of only one syllable, and is easier to pronounce and more pleasant to hear. He kept saying, then, to give his very words: "Hasten, for Crist luve."' A year later, on 12 January 1167 Ailred, surrounded by his friends and fellow monks, whispered his last few words, 'Thou art my Lord and my God, thou art my refuge and salvation, thou art my glory and my hope for ever. Into thy hands I commit my spirit.'

Rievaulx Abbey, founded by the Cistercians in 1131 in the beautiful valley of the River Rye.

The remains of the nave of Rievaulx Abbey church (1140–5). Beyond them, the east end of the church is a masterpiece of Early English Gothic.

ground plan, but the main drain of the redorter, or the 'necessarium' as the Canterbury monks called it, is in good condition. The abbey church can only be described as a magnificent ruin. The oldest section

However, when he was returning to Scotland from a royal mission in 1134, he stayed at Rievaulx and was impressed by the monks' dedication. He made his farewells, but a backward glance at the abbey complex in the valley as he rode away changed the course of his life. His biographer tells us that in a moment of inspiration he turned his horse around and applied to be admitted at Rievaulx as a novice.

His career flourished: he was soon in charge of all new entrants; the abbot sent him to Rome on business; he went with a colony of monks to establish a daughter house of Rievaulx in Lincolnshire; and in 1145 he became Abbot of Rievaulx itself.

While Ailred was ruling Rievaulx, another English monk was called to positions of responsibility in a French monastery, in Provence. Nicholas Breakspeare was Abbot of St Ruf on the outskirts of modern Avignon. But he was destined to sit on St Peter's throne as the first and only English pope in history. However, as a young man his prospects seemed very limited. His father, after a career as a minor royal official, became a monk at St Albans. The family lived at Abbots Langley in Hertfordshire, and a house in the village called Breakspeare Farm may well have been the site of the twelfth-century Breakspeare home. One version of his boyhood has it that he was driven from home in disgrace by his father, but the St Albans chronicler, Matthew Paris, records that Nicholas, trying to get into the abbey, failed a literacy test, and was rejected.

We next hear of him at the monastery of St Ruf where he became an Augustinian canon. By about 1140, the once rejected young Englishman had become abbot. During his frequent

St Ruf

Adrian IV was responsible for a great many building projects during his time in Rome, but nothing has survived. Only in the ruins of St Ruf, in a public park in the suburbs of Avignon, can we see any buildings that remind us of his remarkable career. What is left of the monastery, however, does not attract much attention. Children play among the broken graves of long-forgotten monks in the excavated floor of the nave; a game of boules goes on beyond the line of trees that marks the wall of the church, and a visitor searching for associations with an English pope in the park is a rare event. But the masonry and the craftsmanship, revealed in the carving around the apse at the east end and the tower, would, I suspect, still stand up to the close inspection of St Ruf's most famous monk.

The twelfth-century nave and tower of the Abbey Church of St Ruf, where the only English pope, Adrian IV, served as abbot.

trips to Rome he evidently made an impact on papal officials and, in 1150, he was made a cardinal. The papacy was expanding and he was not the only Englishman serving the pope. The papal chancellor, Robert Pullen, was another. Nicholas proved himself on a mission that may not have appealed to many of his Italian or French colleagues – a visit to Norway and Sweden to establish archbishoprics at Trondheim and Uppsala. After that success he arrived back in Rome just before the death of Pope Anastasius. His name went forward and, with not one dissenter, the cardinals elected him pope.

Nicholas Breakspeare took the name Adrian from a ninth-century pope who had had a reputation as a fighter for papal rights in Italy. Perhaps Nicholas also remembered that the earlier Adrian had granted the monks of St Albans

request to the pope from Henry II. Adrian will always be remembered for the answer he gave. The king wanted papal approval for an invasion of Ireland. Adrian, who wanted to tighten his control of the distant Irish Church, agreed to the plan. The Pope, however, bargained that 'Ireland, of all the islands on which the justice of Christ shines, belongs to the dominion of St Peter and the holy Roman Catholic Church'. That unpalatable condition made Henry pause, but seven years later, in 1172, he crossed the Irish Sea on the strength of a papal Bull issued by an English-born pope to a French-born king.

Henry II and the Murder of Thomas Becket

Adrian IV died before Henry II embarked on his conquest of Ireland. Neither did he live to be involved in the king's challenge to the Church and the martyrdom of Thomas Becket.

Henry II had come to the throne by a circuitous route. A tragic accident had befallen Henry I's son and heir. The boy was drowned at sea and, with no other male heir, Henry I named his daughter, Matilda (William the Conqueror's granddaughter), as his successor. Her husband, the German emperor, had died, so Henry arranged for her to marry Geoffrey Plantagenet, Count of Anjou. But when the old king died in 1135, Matilda and Geoffrey were not on hand, and William the Conqueror's grandson, Stephen, made a successful bid for the throne.

Matilda and Geoffrey took up arms against Stephen, and it took eighteen years of fighting and bitter wrangling before a peace formula for England was arrived at. Stephen finally agreed that Matilda and Geoffrey's son, Henry Plantagenet, should succeed him after his death. By 1154, when Stephen died, Henry had already inherited, and married into, a continental 'empire'. Geoffrey and Matilda had made him

many of the rights and privileges they still enjoyed in the twelfth century. Adrian IV lived up to his namesake. At the beginning of his papacy he had to evict a Roman warlord before he could set foot in the city, and protecting the papal state from predators proved to be a life-long struggle. However, Adrian, in balancing the forces of the German emperor in the north with those of the Norman Sicilian kingdom in the south, proved to be a diplomatic success, at least during his term of office.

He kept in close touch with English affairs, and encouraged and strengthened the English Church. Correspondence flowed back and forth between Canterbury and Rome, as appeals to papal justice became fashionable and frequent among the nobility and the clergy. Adrian had a stream of visitors from England. They included John of Salisbury, the emissary who carried a

Duke of Normandy. Through his parents he had also inherited Anjou, Maine and Touraine, and, by his marriage to Eleanor of Aquitaine in 1152, he had acquired lands that amounted to about one third of modern France. Henry's Angevin empire – the counties, duchies and kingdoms held by the family of the counts of Anjou – made him the most powerful ruler in Western Europe.

In his English realm Henry had become impatient at the growing influence of the Church. Encouraged by Pope Adrian IV, the English Church had become more confident and assertive. A church-state crisis erupted when Henry II put his own man, Thomas Becket, into Canterbury as archbishop.

Becket was the son of a Norman merchant living in London and as a young man he had taken a job as clerk in the household of the Archbishop of Canterbury. There he caught the eye of the king, who promoted him to chancellor. The men got on well together and shared a common interest in field sports and good living, but, on becoming archbishop, Becket began to put the Church's interests ahead of the king's. They quarrelled and Becket was forced into exile. The nub of the wide-ranging disagreement was over the protection that the ecclesiastical courts gave to clergy who had broken the law. The king wanted 'the criminous clerks', having been found guilty by the Church, to be handed over to a royal court official and punished according to secular law. Becket, however, saw this as a form of double punishment.

On his return from exile, Becket railed against his enemies from the pulpit and excommunicated several powerful barons. Excommunication also fell on six bishops whom he accused of usurping his authority while he had been in exile. The bishops crossed to Normandy to complain to the king, who, according to Edward

Grim, spat out these words that led to Becket's murder: 'What miserable drones and traitors have I nourished and promoted in my household, who let their lord be treated with such shameful contempt by a low-born clerk!'

Four of his barons apparently took the king's words as a challenge, and set off for Canterbury, either to arrest Becket, or to do away with him altogether. They arrived in Canterbury on 29 December 1170 and confronted him in the archbishop's palace. Becket was dismissive of their demands and they left shouting threats and abuse. Becket's staff, fearing the worst, persuaded the archbishop to go into the church where he would be safe, but the four knights fol-

Archbishop Thomas Becket, Canterbury's Trinity Chapel.

lowed him in through the north-west transept.

By this time it was late in the afternoon. It must have been difficult to see who exactly was who in the gloomy interior, lit only by clusters of candles. Becket and his monks were all in black and it would have been easy for the archbishop to have made his escape. But he refused to budge. The knights broke into the church and seized him. A scuffle broke out. Watched by a crowd of worshippers, the knights tried to arrest him and drag him outside. Becket resisted; his entourage vanished into the gloom except for Edward Grim, one of his clerks, who hung on to him. He simply refused to let him go. Furious, the knights began to attack him with their swords. Grim, still protecting his archbishop, almost had an arm sliced off by the first blow. As the knights took turns to attack Becket, he fell to his knees in prayer. 'For the name of Jesus and the protection of the Church I am ready to embrace death' are the words he is reputed to have uttered. The third knight, standing over Becket, brought his sword down so hard he removed the top of the archbishop's head and broke his sword. Blood and brains spilled on to the flagstones and 'dyed the floor of the cathedral with the white of the lily and the red of the rose'. Edward Grim relates that the final act of violence came not from one of the knights, but from one of their supporters; a clerk 'placed his foot on the neck of the holy priest and precious martyr, and, horrible to relate, scattered the blood and brains about the pavement, crying out to the others, "let us away, knights; this fellow will rise no more".'

The cathedral monks were stunned and left the body where it was until dawn. Townspeople who had watched the murder 'cut off shreds of clothing and dipped them in the blood'. Others brought phials in which to keep their relic of the archbishop. Meanwhile, some of the monks mopped up what was left of the blood, which they 'poured into a clean vessel and treasured up in the church'. The foundations of an extraordinary cult were laid.

Within a week reports were in circulation in the town of people being cured by touching some of Becket's blood-stained clothes. The blood saved after the murder was put into a large tank of water and cups of the tincture could be drawn off. People bathed their eyes in it, drank it and, as the cult grew, pilgrims could buy little phials of the water to hang around their necks.

Becket's body, hidden for a time from royal officials, was walled up in a tomb that allowed people to lean in and touch the coffin, and pilgrims, bringing their ailments and their anxieties, began to arrive from all over Europe. Canterbury became a centre of pilgrimage; nothing less than the Lourdes of the Middle Ages. With Canterbury's surviving medieval streets, and timber-framed houses, not to mention the crush of modern tourism, it is easy to imagine the hustle and bustle of the twelfth-century city.

But for the English, Canterbury and Becket's shrine have another significance. Like Durham, the cathedral was the burial place of Saxon saints whose graves were staunchly protected by the monks from the unpopular Normans. Even in Henry II's time the Normans were still considered as French-speaking foreigners and it is known that Canterbury was a centre of English resistance. Marginal notes in a twelfth-century psalter show that English was still being written well after the conquest. So the veneration of Becket and the rebuilding of the cathedral to house his shrine were a powerful reminder of a Norman king's crime and a nagging irritation to the Norman establishment. For the English, Becket's shrine was probably both a religious and a patriotic expression.

Canterbury Cathedral

Most of Canterbury Cathedral has been rebuilt since Becket's time. The builders were at work there until the early sixteenth century when the great tower, Bell Harry, rose over the crossing. But the crypt, where Becket was first entombed, is basically Norman. It is a very large space – almost a mirror image of the shape of the church above – and it is the nearest you can get in England to a Norman sculpture gallery. Almost every one of the forest of columns supporting the beautiful vaulted ceiling is carved: spiral fluting and zigzag designs end in extravagant carvings of foliage, animal heads and human faces.

The next twelfth-century point of reference is the north-west transept and the scene of the murder. The place was so sacred in the Middle Ages that they built the new transept without disturbing the floor level where Becket was killed. The spot is now highlighted by a modest shrine that was built in 1982 – a marble-topped table with a modern metal sculpture above, depicting the murder weapons, in the shape of a cross. Set into the original twelfth-century floor, among the other memorials, is a stone slab with the word 'Thomas' inscribed and painted red.

Today's 'pilgrims', one and a half to two million each year, then walk through the late twelfth-century choir and up sixteen steps to the Trinity Chapel at the east end of the cathedral. This chapel was specially built to house Becket's relics, which were moved here in 1220. The building is just like a giant jewel case: a graceful, rounded end, tall marble pillars ending among the intricate ribs of the vaulted ceiling, tall stained-glass windows that fill the walls with colour, and stone tracery. A Gothic masterpiece.

Becket's life and miracles, depicted in stained glass, show the shrine as it was when pilgrims queued up to touch the coffin, collect their holy water from a priest, and hang wax replicas of the parts of their bodies that needed healing around the chapel. An anonymous Venetian traveller in the Middle Ages described the shrine as adorned with

gold panels and encrusted with jewels of every imaginable kind. One ruby was described by another pilgrim as being as big as an apricot – an offering to the saint by the French king, Louis VII, who came to Canterbury to seek healing for his son.

The richly embroidered canopy, which the priests would raise and lower over the shrine, was hung from the same fixing that secures the modern chandelier at the centre of the chapel. The wide expanse of marble floor where the shrine once stood is worn and uneven; it was discovered recently that the floor is made from the steps that pilgrims once mounted to reach the shrine, and that the scalloped gutters in the marble are the result of the feet of countless pilgrims.

Becket's shrine continued to draw the faithful to Canterbury until 1538, when Henry VIII banned all veneration of the saint and had the shrine broken to bits. Several cartloads of treasure were taken away and all that remains of the shrine itself are some fragments of marble which are kept in the cathedral library. The jewel case is empty, and a solitary large candle lights up the shiny, empty expanse of marble where the shrine once stood.

Above: Reconstruction drawing of Becket's shrine, based on the representation in stained glass and on eyewitness descriptions.

Left: The Trinity Chapel. Built in the late twelfth century, it was designed to house St Thomas Becket's shrine, which occupied the central area of the floor under the chandelier.

Right: Canterbury Cathedral crypt. Built in the early twelfth century from limestone brought from Normandy, it is the biggest of the English cathedral crypts.

Henry was said to have been genuinely distressed at the news of Becket's murder. The whole of Christendom was shocked and, under pressure from the pope, Henry was forced to modify his views on clerical matters. 'Criminous clerks' would continue to be tried by Church courts, but in a spirit of compromise the pope agreed that any offences against forest law would be dealt with by the royal courts. It was also agreed that appeals to the papal courts would continue and that all those excommunicated by Becket would have their sentences lifted. Moreover, Henry had to agree to pay for the upkeep of 200 knights to fight with the Crusaders in the Holy Land, and to submit to flagellation in front of Becket's tomb. If nothing else, Becket's martyrdom was an inspiration to other prelates and a warning to secular rulers with tyrannical tendencies.

Henry II's Empire

What an extraordinary lifestyle Henry had! He spent most of his days in the saddle trudging around his empire, which stretched from the Scottish border to the foothills of the Pyrenees. The Angevin kings had no permanent capital or seat of government. The offices of state travelled with the king, along with the court jesters, huntsmen, butlers, grooms and the bearer of the king's bed. The king's chamberlain was in charge of household spending – cartloads of silver pennies trundled along in the baggage train – and the chancellor controlled the king's travelling secretariat. Chancery clerks drew up and issued royal charters and writs, and kept rolled-up copies, 'rolls', of all the outgoing documents.

The chancery was in touch with the English exchequer, which by the 1100s had taken root at Westminster (Normandy had another exchequer and Ireland probably had one as well). An official, often the Archbishop of Canterbury or a secular baron, was appointed 'justiciar' to rule in the king's absence, while provincial and local administration – Henry set up assize courts throughout England – was in the hands of the feudal barons and the sheriffs.

In some ways Henry ran his empire like a family firm. All his sons were given jobs controlling the constituent parts: 'young Henry', the eldest, had been crowned King of England, Duke of Normandy and Count of Anjou in association with the King; Geoffrey was Duke of Brittany; John, Lord of Ireland; and Richard (the Lionheart) ruled the southernmost dominions with his mother, Eleanor of Aquitaine.

Henry kept this disparate empire together by appearing to be everywhere at once, and by the strength of his personality. He was also a competent soldier and an able diplomat. People were in awe of him. His temper at times was uncontrollable and it is said that his grey eyes went bloodshot during rages in which he writhed about on the floor. One curiosity about his empire was his relationship with the French king. In spite of Henry's vast dominions he was a vassal of the French king and had to do him homage for many of his continental possessions. England, to Henry and his Plantagenet successors, was of secondary importance and they spent very little time there – Richard the Lionheart was in England for only a matter of months during his entire reign – and all of them regarded Normandy as the heartland of what was basically a French empire. French tournaments were considered to be superior to English ones and young English knights would cross the Channel to complete their chivalric education and training for the martial arts.

Twelfth-century tournaments were run like a huge war game with combatants galloping across

the countryside in pursuit of each other. Many of them, and probably spectators as well, were injured in the mêlée. Prisoners and captured armour were ransomed for real money.

Later in the Middle Ages the tournament shed its battlefield image and by the mid-thirteenth century it had become a social event which sometimes lasted for days at a time. The knights wrestled, cast stones and lances, jumped long and high, and raced each other across obstacle courses.

Jousting, however, remained the centrepiece of a tournament. Two knights in full armour, shields emblazoned with their arms and helms topped by colourful plumes, would gallop their war horses at each other. The loser would be tilted off by the point of his adversary's lance.

The tournament would end in feasting and dancing in the Great Hall of the castle where musicians, specially dressed for the occasion, played tabors, viols, drums, bagpipes and citoles in the minstrels' gallery. The Lord and his principal guests seated above the salt (the salt was kept in a large boat-shaped dish and anyone not in the Lord's party was seated 'below the salt') would also be entertained by story-tellers, acrobats and jugglers as goblets of wine were passed among the diners.

Troubadour songs from the south of France were popular in England and the adventures of the legendary King Arthur were often recited by story-tellers in castles all over Henry's empire. Indeed Henry II considered himself an authority on Arthur at a time when the conversation of knights all over Europe buzzed with ambition to search for the Holy Grail.

Jonathan Riley-Smith and I could imagine such chivalric speculation taking place after a tournament within the walls of Henry's favourite French castle, Chinon.

The Castle of Chinon

The best view of Chinon is from the bridge over the river down in the town. The tightly packed fifteenth- and sixteenth-century houses beneath the castle walls lead your eye up to the battlements of the castle on top of a rocky spur. From a distance, Chinon Castle looks as if it could still be inhabited but, alas, the roofs were allowed to fall in during the nineteenth century and it is now a romantic ruin.

The castle is really three fortresses, separated by a deep, dry moat cut into the rock. The eastern part, Fort St George, was added by Henry II, but its ruins have yet to be cleared and shored up. The other areas of the castle, however, have been well conserved, including the gate tower at the main entrance.

The slender tower, only 5 metres wide and 22 metres high and topped by a bell turret, contains a small museum dedicated to Joan of Arc. It was to Chinon that the Maid of Orléans came to plead with the Dauphin to lead his army into battle against the English in 1429. There is a fireplace in the main hall of the castle – the only feature of the twelfth-century hall left – where Joan of Arc is supposed to have recognised the French king's son among 300 courtiers and nobles in the large torchlit room.

The victorious Dauphin, as Charles VII, often stayed at Chinon and among the honeycomb of secret passages beneath the castle there is one that led to his mistress's house in the town below.

Chinon, also Henry II's favourite castle, was an

The castle of Chinon overlooking the town on the banks of the Vienne. One of Henry II's favourite castles, it was also where Joan of Arc persuaded the French Dauphin that she should lead his French army into battle against the English in 1429.

The twelfth-century hall where, in 1429, Joan of Arc was received by the Dauphin.

Henry II's effigy at the Royal Abbey of Fontevraud.

Angevin treasury and the treasure tower of Henry's day is still there, along with the massively thick keep. Some of the ramparts show signs of Roman origins, and there are towers set into the curtain wall that retain their twelfth-century vaulted ceilings. It was at Chinon that some of the plotting for the Great Rebellion of 1173 took place. Queen Eleanor, who had encouraged her sons to confront their father, was caught trying to escape from the castle dressed as a man. Henry kept her a prisoner for the rest of his life.

That rebellion, which involved an alliance between Louis of France and Henry's own son, young Henry, failed. But another family quarrel fifteen years later was to end the Angevin's long association with Chinon. Richard the Lionheart, now heir to Henry's empire, and jealous of his brother John, paid homage to Philip Augustus of France and together they marched to unseat Henry. He was forced to agree to humiliating terms and, worn out and dispirited, died at Chinon on 6 July 1189.

From the walls of the castle you can see the road that leads to the Royal Abbey of Fontevraud, about eight kilometres away, where his body was taken for burial. His queen, Eleanor, Richard the Lionheart and King John's queen, Isabel of Angoulême, share with him the twelfth-century Romanesque splendour of the abbey church. And after a lifetime of travelling and war Henry, at least in his effigy – still with some of its original blue, red and gold paint – looks remarkably peaceful.

Baronial rebellion

Richard the Lionheart succeeded Henry II in 1189 and one of his first acts was to release all of Henry's political prisoners, including his mother. But after his coronation at Westminster Abbey on 3 September 1189, the restless and flamboyant Richard was to spend very little time in England. He used the administration, so well tuned by his father, to raise enormous sums of money for his Crusade to the Holy Land. Richard had named his rebellious brother John as heir to the throne, but there was little of the charismatic warrior in John's make-up. Only 1.7 metres tall, and stout as well, John was described as greedy, clever, suspicious and ruthless. But to say that he was perhaps the worst king England ever had is a little harsh. To his credit he maintained and strengthened the royal system of justice established by his father. The Celtic fringe, for example, was never quieter than throughout most of John's reign and, despite war overseas and rebellion at home, the administration continued to function. But he was the king who lost Normandy. The war with France that began in 1202 swallowed up prodigious amounts of money which John raised from a reluctant kingdom. The barons, led by the king's tenants in the north, rebelled against the taxes and refused to fight overseas. They marched south, gathering support, and after London opened its gates to them the king was forced to consider their demands. The conditions he agreed to were enshrined in Magna Carta.

The sealing of Magna Carta did not solve John's problems. Within three months it was rescinded and full-scale civil war broke out. Ruald fitz Alan surrendered Richmond Castle to the king's forces when John himself marched against the barons in the north and, in 1216, the French king's son, Louis, landed in Kent with an

Richmond Castle and Magna Carta

In the years leading up to the rebellion, Richmond Castle played an important role; the hereditary constable of Richmond, Ruald fitz Alan, was one of the leaders of the barons' revolt, and there is enough of the castle left today, especially in the 30-metre-high keep and curtain wall, to imagine the scene as the huge courtyard filled up with troops preparing to confront the king.

The barons and knights who met at Richmond Castle were not only tired of paying for the king's wars; John had soaked them for money in all sorts of different ways – fees for permission for an heir to succeed to his father's estate, the income from property whose owners were wards of court and revenue from bullying widows he was responsible for into marriages that suited his exchequer.

All these abuses were dealt with in Magna Carta, along with many guarantees, including freedom of election within the Church. The two sides met on 'neutral' ground – a meadow called Runnymede on the bank of the River Thames between Staines and Windsor. A portable throne was set up for the king and, in the presence of his counsellors and the representatives of the barons, he put his seal to a document that changed the nature of English government – Magna Carta. But Magna Carta was not just a document of baronial rights. The grandees with Norman names who occupied Richmond and neighbouring castles had included in the sixty-one clauses rights that filtered down from the top to protect townspeople and small landholders as well. The ruling class, which had so recently been forced to choose between their estates in England and Normandy, had begun to think in

invasion force and was welcomed by the barons in London. Driven out of the south-east, King John was marching through the eastern counties drumming up support when he sent his baggage train on a short cut across the 7-kilometre-wide estuary of the River Nene. It is not at all clear what happened, but the horses and wagons with

national terms for the first time. In Magna Carta they began to show themselves as not just representing the Norman settlers but the English as well. Many of the clauses signed by the king at Runnymede are still on the statute book and the charter's famous declaration (clause 39) was enshrined in the American constitution: 'No free man shall be taken or imprisoned or disseized or outlawed or exiled or in any way ruined, nor will we go or send against him, except by the lawful judgement of his peers or by the law of the land.'

Above: *Richmond Castle, Yorkshire. Built in 1071 by Alan the Red, its eleventh-century Great Hall is probably the oldest in England.*

Right: *King John agreed the clauses of Magna Carta in 1215. This version of 1225 is in the British Museum.*

all the goods and chattels of the royal household, including the crown jewels, were lost in quick-sands or surprised and overwhelmed by the incoming tide. John, ill with dysentery, was further weakened by the news and died in Newark Castle on 16 October 1216.

The civil war died with him. But the charter he was forced to agree was reissued and came to be recognised as England's first great constitutional document, leading towards parliamentary government.

CHAPTER FOUR

The Flowering of the Middle Ages

London boasts one of the most magnificent royal mausoleums in the world. Full of gilded tombs, it is a worthy successor to the Abbey of Fontevraud in the Loire Valley as the final resting place of many of the kings of England. It is to be found in Westminster Abbey which was rebuilt two centuries after the Norman conquest. As we took in its splendour, Jonathan Riley-Smith reflected that it was a reminder of the process of anglicisation we had first noticed at Richmond Castle when the nobles, who were equally at home in either Normandy or England, had been forced to decide on one nationality. It is in the reign of Henry III – the builder of Westminster Abbey – that we see how it is not the English who are changing, but their foreign overlords. Although it is another century before we can speak of an English crown and an English nobility, the process has begun.

It is ironic that when Henry III, King John's son and only nine years old, was crowned king in October 1216, London and almost half of England were in the hands of the French. However, a regency council, governing on behalf of the boy, quickly issued a revised version of Magna Carta. Rebellious barons wavered. The focus of their hate, King John, had gone and support for his unsullied son grew. A bloodless victory for the royalists at Lincoln in May 1217 and the capture of a French supply fleet in the Thames tipped the balance; the rebellion petered out, and Louis of France, deserted by his English allies, withdrew.

Henry declared himself to be of full age in 1227, and took control of the kingdom. Intelligent, impulsive, devout and artistically inclined,

but easily led, he was infatuated with the lifestyle and culture of the south-west of France. He surrounded himself with French advisers whose flattery won them many favours and, in 1236, he married Eleanor, the daughter of Raymond of Provence. Her relatives, who followed her to the English court, were given plum jobs and grants of land.

At a parliament in 1248, the barons refused to give the king more money and Matthew Paris tells us, 'he was most severely blamed, and no wonder, for the indiscreet way in which he summoned foreigners into the kingdom and for lavishly and indiscreetly scattering the property of the kingdom amongst them'. The barons resented this greatly. They were also put out when one of the foreigners was secretly allowed to marry the king's sister, Eleanor.

Simon de Montfort

Henry's new brother-in-law was the son of the famous French Crusader, Simon de Montfort, who led the bloody Albigensian Crusade against French Christian heretics in the south of France. The king confirmed de Montfort's claim to the earldom of Leicester and gave him the royal fortress of Kenilworth for life. Henry lived to regret that generous act. He was also to be sorry that he paid no attention to the rising chorus of baronial criticism over royal extravagance. What mattered most to Henry in his fifty-six-year-long reign were the arts; painting, architecture and learning flourished in England with the king's encouragement, and although he would have been the last person to admit it, the culture of his English subjects was beginning to rub off. Although Henry appeared to be no less French

The nave of Westminster Abbey, looking east towards the Confessor's Chapel, built by Henry III in the thirteenth century.

Westminster Abbey

A royal mausoleum is what Henry had in mind when he built Westminster Abbey. Fontevraud, the royal abbey in the Loire Valley, had been lost as a Plantagenet burial site and the need for an alternative, coupled with the king's devotion to St Edward, made the abbey at Westminster an obvious choice.

Edward the Confessor's Norman church, which had been completed in 1066, was torn down and work started on the new abbey in 1245. Its centrepiece was to be a superb shrine to the sainted Anglo-Saxon king. Henry poured money into the project. Fifty thousand pounds, more than two years' royal income, was spent as the very French-looking building took shape. The immensely tall walls with vaults reaching a dizzy 60 metres, supported by double flying buttresses, owed their inspiration to Reims rather than Canterbury. Work stopped when the king died in 1272, and the original Norman nave had to be used until that part of the new church was completed in the sixteenth century. Christopher Wren designed the west towers; they were modified by Hawksmoor and completed in the eighteenth century. But for a building that took seven centuries to evolve, it is remarkably all one of a piece.

The interior, however, is almost obscured by memorials and tombs which jostle for every spare centimetre of floor and wall space. The nave, aisles, transepts and side chapels are packed with the mortal remains of the rich and famous, with a clutter of military heroes, politicians and wistful-looking poets with marbled stares. When you reach the medieval core of the church – the Confessor's Chapel behind the high altar – Henry's concept of a royal mausoleum becomes clear. The Confessor's carved marble shrine is supported on a raised platform in the centre of the chapel, with surrounding side chapels ready to receive royal tombs for centuries to come. And for centuries most of England's monarchs were entombed here.

Jonathan Riley-Smith and I followed the modern walkway, designed to ease the crush of twentieth-century visitors, which takes you on to the raised platform and up to the shrine itself. The carved marble base, with niches where the sick could kneel, looks battered and worn but, unlike Becket's shrine in Canterbury, there is still a substantial amount left to see and touch. A glint of some of the original mosaic work on one of the shrine's corner columns hints at its former splendour, but the golden statues and the precious jewels, as well as the top half of the shrine, all disappeared at the behest of Henry VIII.

Standing by the shrine we were at the heart of the English monarchy. Henry III's gilded effigy, with every whisker of his fashionable beard in place, lies to one side of the shrine, while a plain, grey marble coffin on the other side contains the bones of his son, Edward I. To complete the picture of English kingship the coronation chair, with the Stone of

Above: *Edward the Confessor's shrine. Placed in the chapel by Henry III on 13 October 1269, the carved marble base survived the Reformation.*

Left: *Henry III's effigy in Westminster Abbey.*

Scone (captured by Edward I during his Scottish campaigns), faces the shrine at its western end. The richly carved, and well-worn, chair that was made for Edward I is where English monarchs are still anointed during their coronation.

Henry's magnificent shrine and the Confessor's Chapel never caught the medieval imagination as did Becket's cult centre at Canterbury. More of the shrine survived because of the abbey's special position as England's great national church and royal mausoleum. But veneration of the Anglo-Saxon saint is not entirely moribund. Among the three and a half million visitors who shuffle cheek by jowl around the shrine each year, there are some who make a special pilgrimage to the Confessor's shrine. On 13 October each year, St Edward's Day, they remember Henry III and his Confessor.

than his father, he chose to venerate the last great Anglo-Saxon king and saint, Edward the Confessor, in the building of the sumptuously expensive Westminster Abbey.

Henry was also a compulsive castle builder and is said to have spent £100 000 on castles and manor houses during his reign. Military failures in France also cost a fortune, and poor political judgement helped to foment the dissatisfaction that led to the baronial revolt. Eventually, open warfare erupted. It was now that the king regretted his generosity to Simon de Montfort, the leader of the barons who took to the field against the royalist army. The opposing sides met outside the town of Lewes in Sussex and, in the summer of 1264, Simon de Montfort outmanoeuvred the royal forces and captured both the king and Prince Edward.

With the king obliged to endorse any of his decisions, de Montfort called a parliament in January 1265. Although borough and shire representatives had been summoned to sit with the nobles in Parliament before, de Montfort's summons was for greatly expanded numbers of gentry from the shires and burgesses to represent the towns. It looked like a deliberate great leap forward in the establishment of a future House of Commons, but it was a purely tactical ploy to give his revolutionary government a more convincing veneer of legality.

Modern historians have retreated from describing de Montfort as the far-sighted, altruistic architect of Parliament. Rather, he is seen as the instigator of a novel parliamentary expedient and an opportunist whose arrogance and greed led to his own downfall. In 1265, however, Simon de Montfort was the de facto dictator of England.

Kenilworth

Kenilworth was a handsome gift from Henry III to his brother-in-law, particularly as the king had spent £20 000 on improving the twelfth-century castle. Today it ranks as one of England's most impressive ruins. In the thirteenth century, baronial policy for the kingdom and a new parliamentary structure were dictated here. In de Montfort's time the castle was almost surrounded by an artificial lake that lapped the walls on three sides; you have to imagine those 100 acres of water today, because Cromwell's forces drained the lake, but the original causeway, now standing proud of the meadows, is there.

Kenilworth looks at its best from the causeway; the curtain wall curves away in the distance, and rising above it are the mellow red sandstone battlements of the keep, Great Hall and Tudor apartments. Inside the curtain wall, the castle, like most great ruins, reveals many different stages of development. John of Gaunt, who held the castle from 1361 to 1399, left his mark in the superb range of apartments whose tall elegant windows overlooked the water. The Tudor gatehouse on the town side of the castle is another splendid building. It was turned into a mansion by one of Cromwell's commanders, Colonel Hawksmoor, and is now used as a council chamber by the town of Kenilworth. The Tudor stable block – another building also in good condition – accommodates an English Heritage museum and shop. The part of the castle that de Montfort and the Countess of Leicester would still recognise is the massive twelfth-century keep. It was given bigger windows and a new entrance in Tudor times, and one wall was demolished by Cromwell, but its 6-metre-thick walls and corner towers look as if they might last a thousand years. These great ruined castles rarely give any idea of their domestic life. Kenilworth, however, is different.

The Countess of Leicester's household accounts for part of the year 1265 have survived to give us a vivid picture of everyday life. The accounts, on a parchment roll 6 metres long and 20 centimetres wide, cover expenditure in the countess's three principal residences at the time: Kenilworth, Odiham Castle in Hampshire and that massive fortress, Dover Castle. Like the royal household, the Leicesters were constantly on the move in order to spend some time in each of their castles. The household's top official, and right-hand man to the earl, was the steward. Someone called a 'wardrober', or treasurer, handled all the household funds and kept the earl's valuables under lock and key in the 'wardrobe' – a treasury or strongroom. Another official, also called a steward, was responsible for all the domestic arrangements – a 'major domo' figure like Malvolio, so 'badly used' in Shakespeare's *Twelfth Night*. Simon the cook, Andrew the butler and Ralph the barber all reported to him, along with most of the countess's sixty servants.

The accounts tell us that the laundress, Petronilla, was paid one penny a day, which was noticeably less than the servants who carried the steaming bath water up to their lord and lady. Wax was an important item at six pence a pound. Large quantities were used in the chapel, for lighting and for sealing documents. In the Great Hall it seems as though there was only one big candle burning at the high table.

Oil or tallow lamps, and rushes dipped in tallow, gave additional flickering light in the sparsely furnished hall. There was a dais at one end, chairs for the nobility and, for the rest of the household, benches at trestle tables covered with a white cloth. The main meal was taken in the middle of the day. Beef, mutton, pork, poultry and fish were bought, and presumably eaten, and 'Simon the Fisherman' was sent to the coast to procure porpoise, whale, sturgeon and, during Lent, herring at ten pence for a 'long hundred' (120). The countess reckoned on using 400 to 1000 herring a day during Lent.

When the countess moved the household to another castle, the marshal, who was in charge of the stables and transport, prepared the baggage train. Almost everything went with them; furniture, carpets, stores, the valuables in the wardrobe, the pet monkeys, the harp, were put on carts and pack

Kenilworth Castle, the Warwickshire seat of Simon de Montfort, Earl of Leicester. One of England's most impressive ruins, its walls were once protected by an artificial lake.

horses. The chaplain had a portable altar so that mass could be said along the way, and we can imagine this great retinue with a field kitchen roasting meat over an open fire and unpacking fish and cheese pies, as they picnicked to break their journeys of fifteen or twenty miles a day.

Simon de Montfort's ascendency was shortlived. In August 1265, he was killed by royalist forces at the battle of Evesham. However, the garrison at Kenilworth, still loyal to him, held out against the king. In 1266 the besieging army tried a naval assault on the walls across the lake, but they were beaten off. The siege lasted almost nine months and was broken only when disease and shortage of food brought the garrison to surrender.

Growth of the Towns and the Gentry

Simon de Montfort's parliament of 1265, when representatives of the towns and shires were summoned, clearly demonstrated the growing importance of the towns. Richard I and King John had begun the trend. Short of cash, in the late twelfth and early thirteenth centuries they sold many towns their freedom for an annual rent of between forty and sixty pounds. The royal charters gave the towns the freedom to choose aldermen and full-time officials, to charge tolls, issue licences for markets and hold courts. The king withdrew his sheriff, and the burgesses, who were well-to-do merchants and tradesmen, managed their town's affairs.

It was a flourishing time for towns. Historians' latest estimate is that London had as many as 100 000 inhabitants by the end of the thirteenth century; people with ambition were attracted to the opportunities that the towns offered. The drift towards an urban life gathered pace. To cope with this expansion, after Edward I became king in 1272, many new towns were established by royal decree, not only in England, but also in Wales and Gascony. There, artisans flourished and merchants, particularly those in wool and wine, became rich and powerful. High profits from wool drew Italian merchants to England, but the bulk of the export trade was in the hands

Stokesay Castle

Standing in Lawrence of Ludlow's castle courtyard you would not be surprised if one of his household walked across the grass to greet you. Cosy is the word that comes to mind; the antithesis of Kenilworth. But Stokesay is not lived in today. The family which owned it rescued the castle from dereliction in the early nineteenth century and today the conservation work is continued by English Heritage.

The entrance is across a dry moat and through a delightful Elizabethan gatehouse that dates from the late sixteenth century. Its timbers are richly carved with scenes that include Adam and Eve considering an offer from a Shropshire serpent. The castle itself, across a well-mowed courtyard with a deep well in the middle, has towers at both ends. The middle section contains the Great Hall and the lord of the manor's private apartments. The big difference between Stokesay and earlier English castles is its emphasis on residential rather than military use. In the Great Hall, tall, wide windows – part of the main defensive wall – look out across the moat and flood the hall with sunlight.

Stokesay is a perfect example of castle architecture in transition – from a fortress to an English country house. Much of the timber in the Great Hall is thought to be original and, above the hearth – an octagonal stone in the floor at the southern end – the roof timbers are blackened by smoke. There is no sign of any chimney at any period of the hall's existence.

Everything happened in the Great Hall. Lawrence

of English merchants. They were the men of a new middle class and, having made it in trade, they sought status. They bought country estates and emerged as a new and distinct social class – the English gentry. Lawrence of Ludlow was a typical new country gentleman. The son of a clothier in the Welsh border town of Ludlow, he rose to become an adviser to the king and a substantial landowner.

of Ludlow would have eaten, entertained and held court here, but the emergent gentry were beginning to look for privacy as well. Lawrence built a 'solar' (solarium) for himself: an upper, well-lit room, where the lord and his family could retreat from the rest of the household.

Stokesay's seventeenth-century owners panelled the solar and imported the beautifully carved Flemish oak mantel above the medieval stone fireplace. There are still traces of the red, gold and black decoration of the frieze, and vertical, carved strips of the panelling remain. In the thirteenth century Lawrence of Ludlow would have had his 'wardrobe' in the solar undercroft where the spices, wine, jewellery and plate were kept. In times of stress the family in the solar could quickly reach the three-storey south tower across a drawbridge just outside.

Above: *Stokesay Castle, built by the wool merchant Lawrence of Ludlow in 1291. The gatehouse is Elizabethan.*

Left: *The Great Hall, Stokesay, begun about 1285.*

Right: *The fireplace in the solar at Stokesay Castle; the private apartment of the lord of the manor which adjoined the Great Hall.*

Lawrence of Ludlow's Stokesay Castle typifies not only the rise of the gentry to a position of eminence but also the move of English architecture away from castles as places of defence to homes. However, the peripatetic nature of Lawrence's household, like the Countess of Leicester's, meant that his family was always packing and unpacking all their possessions as they moved around their various estates.

Lawrence himself must have spent a lot of time at the court of the king. The wool merchant was one of Edward I's advisers at a time when the king was trying to establish a monopoly of the wool trade for the crown. Edward, strapped for cash to pursue the war with France that had broken out in 1292, wanted to extract the maximum profit from England's premier export.

On behalf of the crown, Lawrence confiscated

a large amount of wool held by Italian merchants, increased the export duty and 'encouraged' the merchants to lend the king money. A wool fleet was assembled in 1294 and Lawrence of Ludlow sailed on one of the heavily laden vessels bound for Holland where the wool was to be sold. Lawrence drowned when his ship was wrecked off Aldeburgh; his body was recovered and buried at Ludlow, six miles from Stokesay. His descendants, having taken their place among the emergent English gentry, continued to own Stokesay for another three centuries. Such families were to be the main source of knights from the shires who saw it as their duty to attend the king's Parliament.

Parliament

The use of the word 'parliament' goes back much further than Simon de Montfort and his summons to the knights and burgesses in 1265. It was already in common use in France. 'Parlement' described the king's council and gradually clerks and chroniclers on the English side of the Channel adopted the term. By the 1240s it was a familiar term in England that described an amalgam of meetings and functions of royal government. The king met regularly with his great council of baronial and clerical advisers; he also conferred with the officials who ran the household and the exchequer. It must have seemed logical to convene both meetings at the same time of the year, and the joint event, also combined with the king hearing petitions for justice, came to be known as Parliament. Such functions gave the English Parliament its essential difference from the French version – a body of professional jurists who advised the French king.

The royal writ to the sheriffs summoning Edward I's Parliament of 1275 clearly spells out

Houses of Parliament

The opening session of Parliament was usually held in the old Palace of Westminster, a rambling series of buildings begun by Edward the Confessor and developed by the Normans and Plantagenets. Sadly, there is little to be seen of the old palace today. It was gutted by a disastrous fire in 1834 which left only the medieval jewel tower (opposite the House of Lords), the crypt of St Stephen's Chapel (under the House of Commons) and the Great Hall which was built by William Rufus (William II) in 1097. Parliamentary sessions in the fourteenth and fifteenth centuries opened in the Painted Chamber – Henry III's 25-metre-long bedchamber on which he had spent another small fortune in decorations. After the opening, the lords would move to the adjacent White Chamber, later to become the House of Lords, while the commoners met in either the Refectory or the Chapter House of Westminster Abbey.

The first Speaker of the House of Commons was elected in this beautiful octagonal room in 1376. The Speaker's chair was by the central column, a cluster of marble shafts that appear effortlessly to support the eight vaults of the ceiling. About 200 members of the Commons sat on the three tiers of stone benches around the chamber. Henry III's largesse was again responsible for this superb building which was completed in the 1250s. Six great windows, 12 by 6 metres, flood the chamber with light and, below the windows, a continuous arcade of arches with shafts of marble form recesses which are painted with scenes from the Bible. Between the windows and the arcading, the rose makes its first appearance as a royal decorative motif.

The Chapter House, as we see it today, belies the rough handling it has had since the suppression of the monasteries in the sixteenth century. After the monks left it was used as a store for exchequer records, including the Domesday Book. A floor and a gallery were inserted and a new roof was added. The records were moved to Chancery Lane in the City of London in the 1860s, giving Sir Gilbert Scott

The octagonal Chapter House of Westminster Abbey, built by Henry III and completed in the 1250s.

a dangerous opportunity to restore the building. Fortunately, he went about it sympathetically, taking great pains to rebuild the central column and the vaulted ceiling exactly as they had been in the thirteenth century. The glazing is modern, but the tiled floor, watched over by English Heritage guardians who pounce if you stray from the protective matting, is just as Henry III envisaged it. It is one of the best medieval tiled pavements in England. Each tile is fired with different shades of clay and has a complete design. There are King Henry's arms of leopards, wyverns and centaurs, palace scenes, including the queen with a falcon at her wrist, a stag hunt, and musicians with their instruments.

The fourteenth-century Commons met in the Chapter House of Westminster Abbey for forty years. It was a tense time in England's history. Edward III was pursuing the crippling and expensive Hundred Years' War with France. But in the almost circular Chapter House Jonathan and I found it hard to imagine the modern style of the House of Commons, with members shouting at each other. That seemed improbable in a room whose design is not in any way conducive to that sort of confrontation.

But politics in the round was not to last at Westminster. The monks were full of complaints about the members shuffling and stamping and wearing out the floor. They managed to move the debates to the rectangular refectory in 1395. Here members opposed one another directly across the room, and the Commons' permanent chamber was to be the same shape as the refectory. Members moved into the Palace of Westminster in the fifteenth century. Their home was St Stephen's Chapel, with its unaltered choir stalls facing into the middle of the building. Originally a royal chapel of great magnificence, it was destroyed in the fire of 1834, except for a few painted fragments now in the British Museum. In St Stephen's they made speeches across the floor at each other and were kept in order by the speaker, whose chair was in front of the altar. As members came and went they naturally bowed to the altar (rather than the speaker) – a custom that is perpetuated in the modern secular chamber. The refectory and Henry III's St Stephen's Chapel helped to shape the debating style of the modern House of Commons. Standing in the Chapter House today makes you wonder if the present adversarial style of modern political debates could ever have developed had the Commons remained in that elegant octagonal chamber.

who was expected to represent the common people: 'four knights from among those knights of your county who are more discreet and law worthy, and likewise from each of the cities, boroughs, and market towns of your bailiwick, six or four citizens, burgesses or other good men'. They would assemble with the great magnates of the kingdom, along with the king's officials and the princes of the Church. Then, as now, the topic most often at the top of the agenda was taxation. After the signing of Magna Carta it became customary for the king to seek a mandate before setting a new tax.

However, we must not imagine all the Members of Parliament converged on London for their discussions. In the first part of Edward I's reign parliament might be convened anywhere in the kingdom. The gentry and bourgeoisie who trooped off to do their parliamentary duty could find themselves in any one of the king's many palaces or hunting seats, as they might have done in Alfred the Great's day. Only later in Edward's reign was the trend for parliaments to be held at Westminster where the offices of state had come to be based.

As Parliament developed under successive kings some of the men who attended Henry III's parliaments would have been products of the new English universities. Growing prosperity meant an increased demand for more literate and numerate people to fill the growing number of jobs in commerce and in borough and city administration. The burgeoning number of parish churches needed more clergy, and by about 1200 almost every town of any size had a school of some sort. Cathedrals, monasteries and 'colleges' of chantry priests received the licences to run these new educational foundations.

Oxford and Expanding Education

It was usually the sons of nobility who attended these schools. Sons of the emerging middle class were more often taught by entrepreneurial masters who set up their own schools in a house or a hall. Schoolmasters in Oxford (Oxenford), a town that had a reputation for its schools, formed themselves into a masters' guild. And out of that, some time in the second half of the twelfth century, the first English university had begun to emerge, along the lines of existing universities in Bologna and Paris. Many of the masters had studied or taught in Paris, where the university ethos was similar to Oxford, and masters and scholars moved freely between the two institutions.

Oxford's first self-governing college was properly established in 1264 and by the late thirteenth century Oxford had gained a Europe-wide reputation for its teaching of science. Scholars, who had travelled to Spain and southern Italy collecting Arabic manuscripts and translating them into Latin, came to Oxford to teach. They laid the foundations for English pre-eminence in science in the seventeenth and eighteenth centuries. But in the early thirteenth century, tensions between town and gown had led to the dispersal of the university. Masters and scholars left in high dudgeon after being attacked by the townspeople. Some went to Reading and London; others sought temporary accommodation in an unlikely town on the edge of Cambridgeshire's fenland, and, in 1209, laid the foundations of England's second university – Cambridge. But in the Middle Ages Cambridge was to remain the smaller institution and it was Oxford that founded the first of the self-governing colleges that became such an important feature in the development of all English universities.

Merton College

This quadrangle, Mob Quad, would be instantly recognisable to any fourteenth-century scholar at Merton College, Oxford. Little altered, it was the prototype of all English university quads, whose design may have been influenced by the growing popularity of chantry chapels in the twelfth century. Anyone rich enough aspired to have a chantry chapel and a 'college' of priests so that masses could be said for the soul of the benefactor in perpetuity. This very expensive memorial entailed a special chapel built within a parish church, and adjacent accommodation for a number of priests in a 'college' – a quadrangle of apartments with a small communal hall and kitchen. The Kent village of Cobham has a perfect example of a chantry college attached to its parish church.

Such a design fitted the new Oxford colleges perfectly. Walter de Merton, who founded the first one in 1264, was a typical benefactor of the Middle

Mob Quad, Merton College, Oxford; the earliest complete Oxford quadrangle, built between 1308 and 1378. The dormer windows in the roof are sixteenth-century.

Ages. He was self-made, from burgess stock, and rich. He set up Merton College as a place of education for his numerous nephews, but by the time that Mob Quad had been added to the first two buildings (the college chapel and the hall) the intake of scholars went far beyond de Merton's immediate family. Standing in Mob Quad today, taking care not to walk on the grass, you can see the towers of the thirteenth-century college chapel, and in one corner of this otherwise symmetrical complex, the high-pitched stone roof of the college treasury. The first-floor ceiling is made of stone as a precaution against fire.

The young men who strolled around this quad were all studying for a higher degree. It was not until the late fifteenth century that the colleges accepted and taught undergraduates. Merton's scholars would have arrived having already completed the seven-year-long arts faculty course: grammar, rhetoric, logic, arithmetic, geometry, astrology and music. The higher degree at Merton, in law or medicine, took another three to four years, while the students of theology could look forward to about nine postgraduate years – a total of at least sixteen years' study.

Merton's proctors, like all the college authorities, ran a tight regime. Wolves, ferrets, dogs and singing birds were banned as pets; music was allowed only on special occasions when minstrels would be invited to the college; women visitors were strictly chaperoned, and laundresses could have no personal contact with the students. Misdemeanours could attract a flogging, a fine, excommunication, or banishment from the college. Organised games were considered to be a distraction, so the young men cut loose in the town where bear-baiting, card games, singing and dancing, taverns and brothels flourished, despite the strictures of the university chancellor. A riot of 1355 is some measure of the rumbustious nature of the town; tensions between town and gown boiled over into a street battle that lasted for three days and resulted in deaths on both sides and in the sacking of student houses and halls.

Language was another issue that exercised the minds of the scholars and masters of the Oxford colleges. By the end of the twelfth century English had already begun to challenge French and in the thirteenth century the university felt compelled to issue a statute insisting that French instead of English should be used in translations from Latin. English, though, was not to be held back and by the end of the fourteenth century students were reading Chaucer's *Canterbury Tales*, written in English.

Looking at the way in which English developed, it becomes clear that, for a long time in the Middle Ages, the universities, the courts, government offices and large numbers of ordinary people were trilingual, with a command of English, French and Latin. It makes nonsense of the belief that English people and foreign languages do not get on together. Could it be that the later aversion of the English to foreign languages springs rather from a resentment deep in the English character – a collective memory of centuries of oppression by a foreign people who spoke a foreign tongue – the Norman French?

It was not only education that was expanding in the last quarter of the thirteenth century. Young men coming down from Oxford were entering a golden age of prosperity and consolidation. After the political and military shambles of the previous two reigns, Edward I, who succeeded to the throne in 1272, took a firm hold of royal government. Like Henry II before him, Edward was constantly on the move around England, supervising and inquiring. Deeply interested in justice and the law, he produced important reforming statutes every year for the first eighteen years of his reign. A successful Crusader and a diplomat whose ability to adjudicate in disputes between rival states across the Channel was greatly admired, Edward was also a keen sportsman. His prowess at hunting and jousting was legendary and he once sent a wax model of a favourite falcon to the shrine of Thomas Becket in Canterbury in the hope that the bird would be returned to good health.

The Scots and the Welsh, however, have little reason to remember him warmly. He was called 'the hammer of the Scots', and in Wales he snuffed out the remaining vestiges of the Romano-British culture that had taken refuge in the Welsh fastnesses. Then, with Wales firmly incorporated into the kingdom, he embarked on a building programme that was breathtaking in its magnitude and quality. Caernarvon, Conway, Harlech and Beaumaris castles became some of Europe's finest and strongest fortresses, designed to keep the Welsh where Edward wanted them. To further consolidate his position, he planned a programme of new towns, not only in the shadow of his great Welsh castles, but also in England's only remaining French possession, Gascony.

Building in Gascony

That area of south-west France best known to us as the Dordogne was still ruled by the English king in the late thirteenth century. It was what remained of the Duchy of Aquitaine which Henry II had incorporated into his Angevin empire. Bordeaux, on the banks of the Garonne, near its confluence with the Dordogne, was the duchy's capital and the centre of a wine trade that earned the king of England a fortune in customs dues. The wine, of course, was claret – a red wine that is still a very important export from an area with some of the best-known vineyards in Europe. The whole of the hinterland of Bordeaux was given over to vines and the river systems extended the wine-growing areas far into south-western France. The harvest was pressed

Monpazier

Monpazier is almost too perfect. It is one of the best preserved of the English *bastides* in the Dordogne and the main square is delightful. Honey-coloured stone houses, two to three storeys high, surround the main square, which has a well at one end and a sixteenth-century market building at the other. An arcade runs around all four sides of the square, with generous, curved and slightly pointed arches that give access to shops and cafés.

The thirteenth-century church is just off one end of the square, and the court house, which now houses the town's administrative offices, is reached via the arcade at the other. Monpazier, like all the other *bastides* in this area, is a completely planned town based on a grid system of streets with carefully measured plots for the settlers as spaces were filled on the chequerboard plan.

A small number of people came out from England to take up plots, but most were Gascons who were tempted by the offer of freedom from their lord's manorial regime. In the town they had to pay only ground rent – no duties of service to their lord were required. They could amass possessions to which the lord had no right, and they could mortgage or sell their land. The burgesses were free men in every sense of the word, with their own court house and church.

Standing in the arcade of the main square you can look both north and south, along perfectly straight streets lined with medieval houses, to the town gates – the only signs that Monpazier once had walls. This area was close to the French border and Monpazier was defended, but in recent years it has become clear that most of the *bastides* had no town walls. The settlements were not part of some military strategy to fill up the empty land with armed settlers; they were part of the commercial and social change that so characterised the thirteenth century.

The main square of Monpazier in the Dordogne. Established by Edward I in 1285, the town has changed little in the past seven centuries.

in September, and a month later a large wine fleet, laden with wooden casks called tuns, set sail for Bristol, Southampton, Hull and Sandwich – England's main wine ports. It is estimated that England in the thirteenth century imported about three million gallons of wine a year from Gascony, about one third of England's wine consumption.

It was such an important trade that 'tun', the name for the wooden casks in which the wine was shipped, came to be the term used as a measure of a cargo ship's capacity. A tun, which held 252 gallons, took up 60 cubic feet of space in the hold of a ship. From each ship the King had the right to claim 2 tuns if the cargo was 20 tuns or more, plus duty on every drop of the vintage at the production end.

The English had a well-deserved reputation as heavy drinkers. In London in 1309 there were about 350 taverns selling wine at 3d or 4d a gallon. The vintners' taverns, which advertised themselves by hanging branches and leaves over their doors, were usually patronised by the better off townspeople. The poor went to alehouses where the price of a drink in the late thirteenth century was 1½d a gallon for strong ale and 1d for weaker brew. The price was far from cheap at a time when a labourer earned only about 3d a day.

In the early Middle Ages most of England's ale was brewed by women who usually dispensed it in jugs or buckets provided by the consumer. But by the end of the fourteenth century alehouses had evolved into meeting places supplied by brewers operating on a commercial scale. Drinkers could eat, gamble, sing and finish off the evening in the company of a prostitute.

Almost everyone drank alcohol in some form in the Middle Ages and anniversaries and festivals provided an excuse for heavy drinking. The butler of Edward III's household ordered 2000 tuns of wine a year and some of the great baronial households were almost as thirsty. Some even had their own wine vessels to supply their various castles and town houses.

As the wine trade flourished so did the king's plans to expand it even more. Between 1273 and 1307 Edward encouraged the foundation of more than fifty new towns in Gascony – many of which, such as Monpazier, have survived on hilltops and along the banks of the rivers that led to the wine fleets at anchor.

However, the latter part of Edward's reign was dogged by trouble. The death of his beloved queen, Eleanor, in 1290 was perhaps a watershed, and the king, clearly grief-stricken, commissioned a memorial for her which ranks as one of the great works of art of the thirteenth century. Edward spent the modern equivalent of several million pounds on a series of stone crosses to mark the resting places of her funeral cortège en route from Lincoln to Westminster Abbey. Only three have survived, and can still be seen at Hardingstone, Waltham and Geddington.

Rebellion in Wales, and war with Scotland and France, made heavy demands on the pockets of the English, and the king, embarrassingly short of money and unpopular at home, was financing campaigns on three fronts. Still fighting in Scotland, he spent his last winter, 1307, on the border at a monastery near Carlisle. It is said that his last wish was that his bleached bones should be carried to victory against the Scots. But there was no victory and Edward, like his father, was laid alongside the Confessor's tomb in Westminster Abbey.

CHAPTER FIVE

The Age of Chivalry

Records have not survived to tell us how Laxton village in Nottinghamshire coped during the years of famine after Edward died at the beginning of the fourteenth century. It cannot have been easy. To begin with, the countryside was bursting at the seams, with six and a half million mouths to feed. Historians believe that about ten per cent of the population of England may have perished during the famine years. In the unsettled conditions that followed, agricultural production began to decline and expansion stopped.

Manorial records from all over the country show how land changed hands as peasants with smallholdings sold out to their more prosperous neighbours. With produce fetching low prices, many lords of the manor released their villeins and stopped farming their demesnes. They preferred to get what rent they could for the land. But even at the height of the famine the king's tax collectors rode through the countryside seizing cattle and produce in lieu of money. An anonymous contemporary protest song lamented:

> To seek silver for the king I sold my seed
> Wherefore my land lies fallow and learns to sleep
> Since they fetched my fair cattle in my fold,
> when I think of my weal I very nearly weep
> Thus breed many fold beggars,
> and our rye is rotted and ruined before we reap.

The Crises of Edward II's reign

Edward II, who succeeded his illustrious father in 1307, was habitually short of money. The agrarian crisis had a drastic effect on wool production and therefore the king's income from customs dues plummeted. Fighting the Scots and preparing for war with France (which eventually broke out in 1324) soaked up huge sums of money. Edward's infatuation with Hugh Despenser the younger was another expensive indulgence. An earlier infatuation with a young courtier called Piers Gaveston, whom Edward had showered with estates, titles and privileges, had led the king's barons to revolt. They disapproved of the suspected homosexual relationship, and were jealous of the favours bestowed on Gaveston. As a result, the king had been forced to reform his household. Gaveston was arrested and later done away with on a lonely road in 1312 as his captors moved him to another prison.

Looking back on Edward's reign, Jean Froissant wrote in his fourteenth-century chronicle, 'in between two brave and warlike kings, there has always reigned one less gifted in body and mind'. Edward, son of a strong and warlike ruler, was not the king to cope with a spate of natural disasters and war. Twenty-three when he came to the throne; good-looking, but weak and foolish; play acting and a simple country life on the royal estates were what gave him most pleasure.

The young king did not impress the anonymous author of *Vita Edward Secundi*. Summing up the first six years of Edward's rule, he commented, 'He has achieved nothing laudable or memorable save that he married royally [Isabella, daughter of the French king] and has begotten an heir to his crown . . . had he not accepted the counsel of evil men none of his ancestors would have been nobler than he'.

The king's humiliating defeat at the battle of Bannockburn in 1314 presaged a series of natural disasters – not only poor harvest and famine on a scale that no one in medieval England had

Laxton and Medieval Farming

Laxton's farmers have preserved the medieval system of farming open fields divided into furlongs and long strips. In the Middle Ages peasants were allotted strips in various fields so that they could all share the best as well as the least productive land. Some strips or entire fields were then rotated so that in any one year one field in three would be sown with wheat, a second with a spring crop such as barley or peas and the third allowed to lie fallow. Laxton's farmers still cultivate three large fields in this way today and walking along the village street Jonathan Riley-Smith and I could see how the houses, still preserving their medieval alignments, have long personal strips of land at the rear leading to a lane and the open fields beyond.

Life was hard for the villeins or manorial serfs. Before they could cultivate their strips they owed the lord of the manor about two days' work in his demesne, though peasants not bound by service paid rent.

There were many restrictions on a villein's personal freedom: his bread had to be baked in the oven provided by the manor; he had to take his corn to the manorial mill; and no villein could leave the manor without permission. A fee was due to the lord if any of his daughters married outside of the manor – the lord expected to be compensated for the loss of her labour – and even when a villein died the lord could claim a substantial share of whatever had been collected during the deceased's lifetime.

Poaching was considered to be a serious offence – all game and fish belonged to the lord – and cases of adultery were also dealt with in the manorial

Laxton village in Nottinghamshire. Mentioned in Domesday, it is the only village in England where open fields are still cultivated in strips and managed in the medieval way.

court. Offenders in sex trials could be flogged, put in the stocks or excommunicated.

However, the manorial serfs were allowed to gather firewood, berries and building materials on waste land where they also had grazing rights. At Laxton such rights applied to two areas of common land near Laxton village – a right that is still exercised today by the tenant farmers who cultivate the open fields. Indeed, the manorial court that managed the land seven centuries ago still meets

ever experienced, but also awful weather conditions, with harsh winters, storms and floods. It began to seem that they would never improve. One chronicler wrote that people resorted to eating dogs and cats and animal dung; from Alsace in the Rhineland came the story that 'corpses were cut down from the gibbet and eaten'. The

annals of Ulster recorded that 'people used to eat each other, without doubt, throughout Erin'. Disease followed famine and the final torment for the rural population was the death of large numbers of animals from a blight that attached itself to sheep and cattle. Agrarian reforms – particularly the Enclosure Acts of the seventeenth

and carries out many of its medieval functions. Once a year, in late November or early December, the Court Leet convenes in the Dovecot Inn near the parish church, and a jury is appointed to plan the agricultural year ahead. Twelve jurors with a foreman are charged with the responsibility of seeing that each farmer has planted within his allotted strips. The court still has the power to fine today's miscreants, including any inhabitant who does not turn up at the annual court. Office holders, however, confirm that collecting the fine of two pence is difficult!

The 'Laxton Trail', which conveniently starts in the Dovecot Inn yard with a historical display of documents and photographs, took us into a landscape that was lost to England after the enclosures of the eighteenth century. One of the best views of the village, and of the tractors ploughing the ancient strips, can be had from Laxton's Norman castle – one of the largest and best preserved Norman earthworks in the kingdom. The ramparts are 275 metres in circumference and from the tip of the mound you can see the towers of Lincoln Cathedral.

The medieval qualities of Laxton have survived by pure chance. All the fields should have been enclosed, but a dispute between the two most important landowners in the parish prevented this. By the time they had sorted out their difference (not until the 1860s!), the then lord of the manor, Earl Manvers, had run short of money after building nearby Thoresby Hall, and plans to finish enclosing the fields were abandoned. In 1952 the sixth Earl Manvers sold the remaining open fields to the Ministry of Agriculture and since 1981 Laxton has been the responsibility of the Crown Estate Commissioners.

and eighteenth centuries – have made it hard to recreate an impression of life in the countryside as it must have been in those calamitous times. However, Laxton remains as a village in England where the thirteenth-century system of farming is still practised and where the earthworks of a Norman castle and medieval church – and the

village pub! – create the image of a place where time has almost stood still.

But while bad harvests and famine plagued the countryside, it was intrigue that infected the royal court. It was dominated to such an extent by Hugh Despenser (with whom Edward was still infatuated) and his father that finally a coup seemed inevitable. Led by Queen Isabella, it ended with the deposition of the king, the crowning of his infant son, and government in the hands of the queen and her lover, Roger de Mortimer, the first Earl of March. Edward II died at Berkeley Castle in 1327. His body showed no apparent marks, but it was widely rumoured that the murder weapon had been a red hot poker rammed up his anus.

The Black Death

Edward III restored the country's faith in the monarchy, but while England was basking in the euphoria of military victory at Crécy in 1346 (the first major land battle of the Hundred Years War), another enemy was threatening the whole of Europe – the Black Death. It had originated in China in the 1330s. Infected rats had carried the disease to the eastern Mediterranean by 1347 and a year later, after devastating France, the rats arrived at Weymouth port in Dorset on a ship from Gascony.

The plague added to the misery of famine. England, like the rest of Europe, was still weakened by lack of food when the disease took hold of the country. It took two forms. The first, bubonic, was spread by fleas on rats. The results were large swellings around the neck, under the armpits and in the groin. It took a week for the suppurating carbuncles to kill. But the pneumonic version of the plague killed even faster. It was highly contagious, and if an infected person sneezed on you a high fever would take hold.

Ashwell Church Graffiti

Like the bouts of famine, the waves of plague swept all of Europe. England did not suffer alone, but some of the agony the English did suffer during the plague is carved into the soft stone blocks of the north wall of Ashwell church tower. A few lines in Latin start with a matter of fact statement, 'the first plague was in June 1349'. Underneath, on the next course of masonry, the word 'pestilence' is followed by more words that become steadily larger as the terse message unfolds: '1350, a pitiable, fierce violent (plague departed), a wretched populace survives to witness'.

Ashwell Church, Hertfordshire. Graffiti on the wall of its fourteenth-century tower recall the trauma of the Black Death which devastated England in 1348.

Those few lines, perhaps because they are carved in stone, have enormous impact. They convey the agony, terror and frustration of someone who survived. On parchment, chroniclers added more detail: 'Men and women carried their own children on their shoulders to the church and then threw them into a common pit.' William of Dene, a monk from Rochester, must have witnessed such scenes himself: 'From these pits such an appalling stench was given off that scarcely anyone dared ever to walk beside the cemeteries'.

Many churches were left without priests, cattle roamed through the unharvested crops and streets of houses stood empty in the towns. In some villages there were barely enough people left to collect and bury the dead. A calamity on that scale is hard to comprehend, but the plague only paused. Eleven years later it was back again, accompanied by violent storms, 'and in the end a mighty wind, Mauris, thunders in this year of the world, 1361'.

This final inscription on the wall of Ashwell church tower refers to the great gale in January of that year which blew down the spire of Norwich Cathedral and may account for the fact that Ashwell's own tower was rebuilt about twenty years later. Even in the peaceful churchyard, with a spring that feeds the headwaters of the river Cam at the bottom of the rectory garden, the torment of the plague is not far away. As Jonathan Riley-Smith and I left the church by the main door we looked to the right. Under the grass, victims of the Black Death lie buried – in a plague pit.

Two to three days was the most you could expect to live. The playground rhyme, 'Ring a ring a roses, a tishoo, we all fall down', stems from the plague and would have struck terror into the hearts of medieval Englishmen. No community escaped, however remote, and at the village of Ashwell in Hertfordshire there is a diary of the course of the plague that still chills the spine, scratched on the wall of the parish church.

After each bout of plague – it recurred every ten years until 1390 – those left behind stepped into dead men's shoes; labour was at a premium. Richard II's government tried to hold down wages and control prices, but such measures could not stop the dramatic change that was taking place in rural communities.

The trigger for revolt was an increase in the poll tax in 1381 to pay for the war in France. Leading a truly popular uprising, Wat Tyler marched on London and, in a celebrated encounter with Richard II, won from the king a charter of peasant rights. The king rescinded the charter as soon as his troops could regain the initiative from the mob, and the rebellion was put down. But the incident, which showed great courage on the part of the boy king, is remembered as one of very few positive features of Richard's reign. He met the same end as his great-grandfather – deposition and murder.

War in France

A popular way to escape from political instability, famine and plague at home was to fight the king's war in France. Since 1337 English armies had been in action because of a dispute over Gascony – which England continued to hold as her last remaining possession in south-west France. The duchy was not 'sovereign' territory. Since the middle of the thirteenth century it had been held by the English crown as a fief of the French king. English monarchs therefore had to pay homage for the duchy, and part of that feudal relationship obliged the fief holder to provide knights as required to fight the French king's wars. And although Gascony was governed by English nobles appointed by the crown, any Gascon had the right of appeal to the French king's court as his feudal overlord. The whole situation was fraught with opportunities for dispute and when Edward III refused to pay homage to the French king in 1337, Philip of France announced that he would confiscate the duchy. Edward retaliated by laying claim to the French throne and both sides enthusiastically launched into a war that was to last for more than a century. In France it was to become known as the Hundred Years War.

The nobles who rode to battle in the Hundred Years War saw themselves as knights in shining armour. It is probably not too harsh to describe them as puffed up and prickly with honour,

pride, aggression and their social position. Their ideas of chivalry came from such ceremonies as the initiation of knights, when they were dubbed wearing a scarlet mantle and a white belt after an all night vigil in the church. The knight's sword was blessed and he vowed his allegiance to his lord, to the Church and to protecting the weak, the fairer sex and, above all, his honour.

Enormous trouble was taken over the knights' coats of arms, which were emblazoned on surcoats and shields. Heralds, who were armorial experts, presided over tournaments and had a special 'neutral' status as messengers on the battlefield where they would also have to identify the dead from their insignia. But during truces in the war, knights from different sides were happy to take part in competition together.

The slaughter of the common soldiery, mercenary groups out of control among villages and towns, and the 'scorched earth' policy of English armies in France seemed to touch the chivalric nobles lightly. They all shared in the romantic ideals of King Arthur and his knights of old, and it was Edward III who founded an Arthurian society which met in the Great Hall at Winchester. The huge oak table-top in the hall is traditionally the table Edward had built for his knights. He also founded the Order of the Garter, which is said to have gained its unusual emblem during a victory ball in Calais in 1347. One version of the story is that the king, dancing with a pretty woman, saw her garter come off. He gallantly picked it up, wrapped it around his own knee, and declaimed, 'Honi soit qui mal y pense'.

To imagine what life must have been like both for the knights and for other troops caught up in this war, we made our way through the vineyards of Bordeaux to the medieval castle at Villandraut.

Villandraut

This massive square castle of Villandraut has something familiar about it. The design, with its huge drum towers and moat, is remarkably like one of England's most famous and picturesque castles, Bodiam, in Kent. Villandraut almost certainly had an influence on English castles in England and Wales. One distinctive feature is the absence of a central keep. Villandraut's equivalent is the main gate flanked by two formidable drum-shaped towers, with a 5.5 metre deep moat to complete the defences.

There is little left of the buildings – roofs are off and walls broken down – that once occupied the almost square castle courtyard. But five of the six drum towers are in good condition, including the interior staircases that take you in spiralling darkness to the chambers at various levels and out on to the battlements at the top. In one elegant, but cold, vaulted chamber we visited, which still has some of its paintwork on the walls, the bosses of the rib-vaulted ceiling are carved with the arms of Pope Clement V.

The first of the Avignon popes, he was born in a manor house where the nineteenth-century church now stands in the village. The pope's much vandalised tomb is only 4 kilometres away in the cathedral-like church of Uzeste. He wrote to one of the English kings saying that he was going back to Villandraut for some peace and quiet, and no doubt he found it in that chamber, looking out across the magnificent vineyards that made the duchy such an important prize.

Unlike the French, the English soldiers who paraded in the courtyard of Villandraut were professionals paid by the day. A duke was contracted at thirteen shillings and four pence, senior officers (commanding up to thirty knights) received four shillings, knights two shillings, men at arms (esquires) one shilling, and foot soldiers two pence a day. It was good money at a time when an acre of arable land cost four pence, and a ploughman took home twelve to thirteen shillings a year. The remarkably successful Welsh archers, whose prowess at Crécy and Poitiers had won them international fame, were paid a handsome six pence a day. Their arrows, loosed from yew or oak bows, were first seen in France at Crécy and were capable of piercing armour at a range of about 230 metres. An archer could shoot ten to twelve arrows in a minute compared with only two or three from the crossbow favoured by the French and their Genoese mercenaries. And the effect of a sky full of metal-tipped shafts descending on an enemy was catastrophic. For a time the English were invincible and, bursting with patriotic pride, Englishmen showed no reluctance to fight for the warrior king Edward III or his equally warlike son, the Black Prince.

Soldiers, of course, went to war not only to fight, but also to share in the spoils of war, and officers, whose estates at home were often suffering from low rents and high wages, stood to gain a fortune from the ransom of prisoners. Four figures for a captured French noble were not uncommon. The Black Prince netted £66 000 for fourteen knights and nobles after Poitiers, and the unfortunate French king, John, captured and taken to the Tower of London, was priced at half a million pounds.

If you have a head for heights a volunteer from an archaeological group will guide you up on to the battlements of the castle of Villandraut to do a circuit of the old Gascon fortress 20 to 25 metres above the moat. Up there, on Villandraut's battlements today, Jonathan Riley-Smith and I appreciated how difficult the castle would be to

Left: *The castle at Villandraut, south-west France. Built in 1306, it guarded the south-western approaches to the capital of Bordeaux in English Gascony.*

Right: *Interior of Villandraut; some of the vaulted rooms in the towers still have traces of decoration.*

take, with the defenders shooting down arrows and, from the towers, picking off targets with their ballistas – giant crossbows that fired metal arrows that could skewer several soldiers at a time. Red hot sand rained down, boiling oil was tipped on the attackers and bales of burning straw and Greek fire assailed the ramming and siege tower parties.

Villandraut was one of several fortresses that stood between the *bastides* of the hinterland and the capital of Bordeaux. It was the last English castle to surrender, in July 1453, but the only serious damage to the walls seems to have taken place in 1592 when the French king, Henry IV, was besieging the castle.

Far left: *Gilt bronze effigy of Edward III (father of the Black Prince) in Westminster Abbey. The face was probably modelled from a cast taken after the king's death.*

Left: *Edward the Black Prince. The famous effigy is in the Trinity Chapel of Canterbury Cathedral.*

Malbork Castle

The view of the castle, as you arrive across the flat Vistula delta plain, has hardly changed since the Middle Ages. From as far away as 12 miles you can see the towers and high-pitched, red-tiled roofs of this vast brick castle. The Poles claim that Malbork (Marienberg as it was known to the Teutonic knights), covering some 20 hectares, is the biggest brick-built castle in the world; like Jonathan Riley-Smith, I found it hard to disagree with them as we explored courtyards and buildings that combined the functions of monastery, arsenal and capital, for what was virtually a self-governing crusader state, licensed by the pope.

The medieval entrance to the castle was by a bridge across the sluggish, green waters of the Vistula tributary, the Nogat, and through the gate guarded by two large drum towers with conical roofs. The walls, with a moat on three sides, enclose a rectangle which stretches for almost a third of a mile along the river. Inside, Marienberg is really three castles in one. First is the high castle, which was the inner core of the fortress. Here were the monk soldiers' refectory, chapel, dormitory and chancery. We had to cross a dry moat to get to the middle castle where there was accommodation for visiting knights, the Great Hall and the Grand Master's palace. The third section, the outer bailey, beyond further defences, had stabling, a bakery, a brewhouse, workshops, a church and servants' accommodation. Many of the buildings in this part of the castle are still waiting to be repaired as part of a conservation project that will take generations of craftsmen to complete. Much of their effort has been to restore the damage done during World War II. The Germans were ensconced in the castle and had their ammunition dump in the medieval

Left: *Thirteenth-century Malbork (Marienberg) Castle, headquarters of the Teutonic knights in Prussia. Crusaders from all over Europe feasted after battles against the pagan Lithuanians.*

An architectural detail of Malbork Castle – Europe's largest brick-built fortress.

Knightly Chivalry

During gaps in the Hundred Years War chivalric knights from all over Europe were tempted away to another theatre of war – the Northern Cru-sades, which were organised by the Teutonic knights. The Teutonic knights were a military order founded in 1190 by German merchants during the Crusades to the East. The knights, like

church. Russian bombardment of the eastern side of the castle lasted two months and inevitably the church, which suffered a direct hit, was badly damaged.

The crusading package that attracted chivalric knights from all over Europe included a few weeks of operations against Lithuanian pagans followed by feasting, jousting and prize-giving in great style. The Teutonic knights, who had redirected their crusading efforts to the Baltic after the Holy Land had been lost by Christendom, were successful enough in their advertising to attract such illustrious princes as Henry Bolingbroke. Before he usurped Richard II in 1399, the future Henry IV went twice to Marienberg. Once he took with him a large retinue which included thirteen knights, eighteen squires, three heralds, ten miners and engineers, and six minstrels. Henry was a big spender. The £4360 he got through must have been a handsome windfall for the Teutonic knights' treasury.

In the fourteenth and fifteenth centuries, grooms would have prepared the knights' horses in the outer bailey for the summer and winter 'reysen'. Just before Christmas, knights would arrive for a short campaign of three to four weeks. The idea was to stage surprise raids on Lithuanian villages and towns, kill or capture as many pagans as possible and carry off any portable loot before a counter-attack could be organised. It was a demanding sport even for hardened campaigners from France. The northern winter could suddenly thaw and send heavily armoured knights crashing into ice-covered rivers and bogs. The chances of dying of exposure or of being lost in the trackless wilderness were not to be ignored.

A 'sommer-reysa' was a full-blown military campaign lasting several months rather than weeks, when commanders sometimes made use of the Teutonic knights' navy to bring siege machinery upstream from the Baltic ports. Summer objectives were to encroach on pagan territory and hold it by building forts and new towns with churches as bases from which to convert the reluctant natives. At times when pagans were worth more alive than dead, wagon trains returning to Marienberg often brought in thousands of slaves.

At the close of each crusading campaign the knights would assemble in Marienberg's middle castle and, after washing their hands in the stone basin that you can still see outside, they would file into the Great Hall for an end-of-reysa feast. Tangible evidence of the splendour of the feast came when the German occupying army discovered a hoard of silver goblets. The hall, which adjoins the Grand Master's palace, is one of the best preserved parts of the castle. It is a room lit by tall Gothic windows; 9 metres above, the palm-shaped plasterwork of the vaulted ceiling is supported by three elegant columns.

The original fourteenth-century heating system has survived. Hot air, carried by pipes all over the building, wafts into the Great Hall through a series of discreet brass grilles set into the floor. When it was tested in the nineteenth century the system was still effective in temperatures that plummeted to between minus 15 and 20 degrees centigrade.

In this cosy aftermath of pagan massacres, the outward show of chivalry flourished; there would be feasting and speech-making and, under the colourful banners of knights who had 'reysed', the Grand Master would award badges of merit to those who had distinguished themselves in battle.

all the other military orders, were forced to leave the Holy Land after the collapse of the Crusader kingdom of Jerusalem and in 1309 the Grand Master settled in Prussia. Twice a year these northern knights advertised a crusading 'package' based on their great castle of Marienberg (Malbork) and the Baltic port of Danzig (Gdansk).

Bolton Castle

Bolton Castle, Yorkshire. Built in the late fourteenth century, it was the seat of the Scrope family.

Built around a central courtyard, Bolton Castle is more of a palace than a fortress, but the main gate is still equipped with two portcullises and 'murder holes' through which to shoot any intruders who might have penetrated the outer defences. Across the courtyard, to the right of the gate, is the Great Hall. Not as spacious as that of Marienberg, it is open to the sky now, but standing in what was the undercroft you can look up to where the floor and ceilings would have been.

The seventeenth-century antiquarian, John Leyland, who described the once-splendid hall, wrote that 'the smoke from the (central) hearth was wondrously conveyed by means of tunnels through the walls and by no other louvres'. The flues he referred to are just above the window openings;

One of the English families who we are almost certain went to Prussia and feasted in the Great Hall at Marienberg is the Scrope family. Some of the sons and nephews of the first Baron (Richard) Scrope no doubt came back with badges of merit. Looking down from the battlements of Bolton Castle – their home in North Yorkshire – I could imagine them returning along Wensleydale to celebrate, this time in Bolton's Great Hall. The castle must have looked magnificent as the young Scropes rode up the valley; a great square building rising to more than 30 metres at the top of its four towers, and gleaming in the sunlight from a fresh coat of whitewash.

We know how seriously Lord Scrope took chivalry in the last half of the fourteenth century, from the surviving records of a five-year court case over his right to wear a particular crest. A knight called Sir Robert Grosvenor and Sir Richard Scrope both claimed the design of a crab emerging from a coronet, and the Court of Chivalry, where armorial disputes are still heard, visited churches and castles where the knights displayed their coats of arms, and called a large number of witnesses who had seen the Scropes in action in Prussia, France, Hungary and the eastern Mediterranean. Geoffrey Chaucer testified for Scrope and it is more than likely that Chaucer's Knight, in the prologue to the *Canterbury Tales*, is modelled on the Scropes.

> Ful worthy was he in his lordes werre,
> And thereto hadde he riden, no man ferre,
> As wel in cristendom as in hethenesse,
> And ever honoured for his worthynesse.

there was a minstrels' gallery and at the east end of the hall two doorways, which you can still see, led to the kitchen and the butteries. Lord Scrope's will tells us that there were tapestries with griffins woven in metals, table cloths for seven tables, salt cellars and chalices.

The chapel at Bolton Castle, on the second floor above the malting house, was turned into a chantry chapel in 1399 – the year that Henry Bolingbroke deposed Richard II. The loyal old baron paid for six monks to pray for Richard's soul every day in perpetuity. As in other great houses, the monks would have given lessons, including French as a second language, to the sons of the local gentry who were sent to the big house to be educated in courtesy and chivalry.

The castle has been ruinous since its destruction by Oliver Cromwell's Parliamentary forces in 1647. It is, however, still owned by a branch of the Scrope family that built it and, with the help of English Heritage, the Hon. Harry Orde-Pawlett has embarked on a programme that is gradually closing the gaping cracks in the masonry and removing well-rooted scrub from the battlements. Bolton is shaking off two and a half centuries of neglect and isolation and resuming her medieval grace and grandeur at the head of Wensleydale.

At Alisaundre (Alexandria) he was when it was
    wonne.
Ful ofte tyme he hadde the bord bigonne
Aboven alle nacions in Pruce (Prussia);
In Lettow (Livonia) hadde he reysed and in Ruce
    (Russia),
No Cristen man so ofte of his degree.
In Gernade (Granada) at the seege eek hadde he
    be
Of Algezir (Algeciras), and ridden in Belmayre
    (Morocco).
At Lyeys (Ayas) was he and at Satalye (Antalya),
Whan they were wonne; and in the Grete See
    (Mediterranean)
At many a noble armee hadde he be.

In this poem, Chaucer's Knight campaigns wherever a war or a crusade is under way, and although some Chaucerian scholars believe that the poem is contemptuous of an outdated mercenary, it is perhaps more likely that Chaucer is accurately reflecting the chivalric aspirations of fourteenth-century society. Scrope, who won his case, had lived through a century that had seen a major social change in England. A population that had been halved by famine and plague had seen off serfdom and opened up the rigid class structure. Chaucer himself was an example of social mobility. His great-grandfather had been a peasant, his father a merchant in London, and the young Chaucer had risen to become a member of Prince Lionel's household. He married a lady-in-waiting of the queen's household and pursued his literary career while undertaking diplomatic missions for the king. In the 1370s he became a Controller of Customs in London.

Chaucer was the first poet to breach the dam that was holding back the English language. Whereas his predecessor, John Gower, had written in French, Latin and English, Chaucer was the first poet to write solely in English. Such was the move towards English in the fourteenth century that grammar schools all over the kingdom were translating their Latin texts into English.

Whatever the reason, French and Latin were becoming displaced. English was taking over. One explanation for ruling families like the Scropes being keen to take up English as their first language was surprisingly simple. Like Chaucer's prioress in the *Canterbury Tales* who 'spoke the French of Stratford atte Bowe, the French of Paris she did not know', the English gentry were speaking provincial, Norman French. It sounded amusingly provincial in Paris; they were laughed at and patronised and, by the end of the fourteenth century, the English had retaliated by refusing to speak French at all. It is an intriguing thought!

Battle of Tewkesbury

Left: *Tewkesbury Abbey, Gloucestershire. Completed and consecrated in 1121, it is one of the largest parish churches in England.*

Right: *The sacristy door lined with pieces of armour scarred by the battle.*

Two exhausted armies faced each other on the morning of 4 May 1471. Both sides had marched in full armour all the previous day. Queen Margaret's Lancastrians were attempting to join up with sympathetic lords in Wales, while King Edward's army was determined to stop her fording the River Severn. The exact location of the first part of the battle is still disputed by historians, but the battlefield itself is still largely open country and probably has not changed appreciably in five centuries. The high ground nearest the imposing Abbey of Tewkesbury on the southern side is most likely to be where the Lancastrians took their stand. With 6000 troops they had a small advantage in numbers. From a distance of only about 350 metres, the Yorkists opened with an artillery barrage. One section of the Lancastrian forces rushed down the slope and engaged the enemy in a hand-to-hand mêlée that made no distinction between men-at-arms and nobles. The counter-attack failed and, as the Lancastrians retreated, spearmen on their flank wreaked more havoc.

The main Lancastrian army, apparently demoralised at the way things were going, broke ranks and began to retreat, pursued by the Yorkists. Some escaped through the town; others swam to safety across the Severn, but large numbers died in a field that still bears the name 'bloody meadow'. Between 1500 and 2000 are believed to have perished and, among them, the teenage pretender to the throne, Prince Edward.

After the battle, soldiers streamed into the sanctuary of Tewkesbury's great Norman abbey. Jonathan Riley-Smith and I easily imagined the defeated Lancastrians crowding into the beautiful nave, some wounded, all exhausted and all hoping

The Wars of the Roses

The world of knights and chivalry, so enjoyed by Scrope and Chaucer, came to an end during the Wars of the Roses. They were so named because both sides chose the same emblem – a rose: red for the Lancastrians and white for the House of York. Henry V's premature death, in 1422, had left his baby son as king of both England and France. But Henry VI grew up to see his father's empire shrink away. Calais became the last remaining English possession on the mainland.

Dissatisfaction with Henry VI's reign – he was said to be unworldly, incompetent and, at various stages, mentally unstable – drew a challenge for the throne from John of Gaunt's grandson, Richard of York. Noble families took sides and

Jonathan (left) and the author (right) at the scene of the worst fighting.

for mercy. The king arrived and in a mood of euphoria pardoned everyone in the church, but the Lancastrian lords were not to be spared. The king changed his mind and had them executed.

The abbey, a lucky survival from the suppression of the Tudor age because the people of Tewkesbury offered Henry VIII the money he would have got from selling the lead on the roof, has two poignant memorials of that day in May 1471. The first is the diamond-shaped plaque near the altar where Prince Edward is buried. The second is a surprising survival of the battle in the sacristy of the church. The door is heavy to open. Nailed to the back of it are pieces of armour collected from the battlefield – some of them scored by sword and axe blows, and others pocked with the bulges and frayed holes made by gun shot – a poignant reminder of the ferocity of the battle.

civil war erupted at the battle of St Albans in 1455. Richard of York, who was killed at the battle of Wakefield in 1460, was succeeded by his son who, after his victory at Towton Moor, was declared King Edward IV in 1461.

During this time, the deposed King Henry VI and his son Prince Edward were still alive – Henry in the Tower of London and Prince Edward in France with his mother, the formidable Queen Margaret. From exile in France, she returned with her Lancastrian prince to win back the throne. At Tewkesbury in Gloucestershire, her army and the Yorkist king's forces met for what turned out to be a decisive battle. The Lancastrians were defeated and at Tewkesbury not only did the flower of Lancastrian nobility die, but chivalry had run its course at well.

When the victor of Tewkesbury, Edward IV, died his eldest son was crowned King Edward V and reigned for two months. The boy-king and his nine-year-old brother, Richard, were entrusted to their uncle, Richard of Gloucester, Protector of the Realm during Edward's minority. But after 1483 the young princes were never seen again. Their uncle had shut them up in the Tower and their death remains a mystery. In 1674 bones of two children were discovered in the Tower and a casket containing the remains can be seen in Westminster Abbey. It is believed that the wicked uncle of Shakespeare's drama was indeed responsible for murder. Richard had himself crowned as Richard III in 1483 and his brutal rise to power and his unpopular reign led to the battle of Bosworth and Henry Tudor's appearance in England's story. Descended through his mother from John of Gaunt and Catherine Swyneford, Henry defeated Richard in hand-to-hand combat on Bosworth field in August 1485, and is said to have plucked the crown from a thorn bush where it had rolled after Richard's fall. The long line of Plantagenets, that had begun with Henry II in 1154, had ended, pushed out of history by the Tudors, who were to preside over a profound social upheaval – the Reformation.

CHAPTER SIX

Gloriana's Protestant Patriots

While the houses of York and Lancaster were attempting to slaughter each other, most people were only on the sidelines of the conflict and, despite everything, English merchants were doing good business, even expanding. The English economy still rode on the sheep's back.

Wool, the major export of the fourteenth century, was still important, but, instead of shipping only raw material, England's looms were turning out enormous quantities of cloth for export. This trade developed to such an extent that by the end of the fifteenth century, it seemed as if all of Europe was dressed in English cloth. Italian merchants, for example, took it in exchange for such imports as sweet wines, silks, velvets, spices, sugar, fine Milanese armour and dyes for the cloth industry.

The bulk of England's woollen exports were handled by two competing associations. The first were the Staplers, wool merchants who were given a monopoly to export the bulk of the wool clip via Bruges. The Staplers shipped the wool, collected the customs dues for the king and loaned him money in return for their monopoly. After their move to Calais in continental Europe (England's only remaining foothold in France, captured initially by Edward III in 1347), they also paid for the cost of maintaining the garrison there. As the trade in unspun wool began to decline in the late fourteenth century, they added cloth to their warehouses. That put them in direct competition with the Merchant Adventurers, the other main group of merchants, mainly from London, Ipswich, Newcastle, Bristol and York.

The Merchant Adventurers

Merchant Adventurers' Hall, York. Built in 1357, one of the oldest guild-halls of its kind in Europe.

The Company of Merchant Adventurers of the City of York still meet in their fourteenth-century hall on the bank of the River Fosse. The merchants' business has changed but their meeting place is much the same. Built in 1357, it is a superb survival of fourteenth-century architecture. The only substantial changes made to the original structure are the sash windows put in during the eighteenth century; the hall's great oak-timbered roof, supported by two central pillars, covers an area of some 25 metres by 18 metres.

The Company of Merchant Adventurers was not a company in the modern sense. Each of the Adventurers traded, and took commercial risks, on his own account, and used the 'company' like a craft or trade guild to provide a framework of regulations. For example, rates of pay, hours of work, trading strategy and the chartering of ships

Although many English Merchant Adventurers grew rich, they never achieved the wealth and status of the Italian merchant community whose sophistication in banking was far in advance of any English merchant. English mercantile activity, reassessed by modern economic historians,

Interior of Merchant Adventurers' Hall.

At home, the company, like all the medieval guilds, played its part in the spectacular pageants and cycles of Mystery plays that were a feature of the guilds. Most guilds were also involved with charitable work and had a strong religious background. The Merchant Adventurers were first known as the Fraternity and Guild of Jesus Christ and the Blessed Virgin Mary. Their religious and charitable interests are clear in the undercroft of the hall, where there is a chapel. When it was built in the fourteenth century it had three stained-glass windows, two hand organs, five altars and, according to the company archives, many beautifully carved images. Priests, paid for by the merchants, conducted services and took care of any resident pensioners, or dependants of merchants who had fallen on hard times. In 1835, a report of the Parliamentary Commissioners described the Merchant Adventurers' hospital in the undercroft of the hall as having accommodation for five poor men and five poor women. 'They receive an allowance of £2 every month called court money, and allowances of 10 shillings at Christmas, at Easter, and at Whitsuntide respectively called good time money, and the whole equally divided among them.'

Captains of industry and commerce in York today continue to appoint a governor who, sitting on a dais in the main hall in a beautifully carved eighteenth-century stall, holds court, with the company's mace on a desk in front of him. No longer are the members deliberating on trading matters. That ended in 1827. And there are no poor people in the hospital. Instead, the company contributes to outside charities, and it is committed to the maintenance of its magnificent building which is a unique part of England's trading history.

were company matters, dealt with by members meeting in their hall. The merchants were fussy about who joined. No 'vulgar pedlars' (shopkeepers) need apply, and those young men who were admitted had to face a seven-year apprenticeship. At their main base in Antwerp, and at other foreign ports such as Danzig on the Baltic, the company had its own compounds, which were like self-governing colonies. 'Company law' was administered by a merchant governor whose stringent regulations had to be obeyed. There was no staying at taverns or inns of ill-repute; no gambling or drinking to excess; no swearing or fighting. Attendance at church services was obligatory, marrying foreign women was not allowed, and at all times the merchants had to show respect to their governor and to behave in a way that would not imperil the company's status abroad.

appears to have been muted. English merchants may have controlled more than fifty per cent of England's cloth trade, but they passed up the opportunity to exploit the trade beyond their traditional markets in the Low Countries and the Baltic.

The Wool Trade

Much of the cloth that kept the merchants in business was produced, not in the towns, but in the countryside. Towards the end of the thirteenth century, fulling mills had begun to take over from the traditional treading of the cloth in

Lavenham

Lavenham was one of those lucky towns which escaped the bout of mindless and greedy redevelopment of the 1950s, 1960s and 1970s. This sleepy East Anglian town owes its survival to 150 years of neglect and isolation after the decay of the cloth-making and spinning industries that had sustained it. Commercial developers saw no profitable future here and, as a result, anyone in search of a late medieval town is immediately impressed by street after street of timbered houses, all built in the fifteenth and sixteenth centuries.

Two guildhalls survive in Lavenham: the Wool Hall which was built in 1446 and is now part of the Swan Hotel; and the Hall of the Guild of Corpus Christi on the south side of the market place. Now managed by the National Trust, its rambling interior, full of creaking staircases and sloping floors, houses a collection of equipment and documents that trace Lavenham's history as a weaving town.

What a boom town Lavenham must have been. From an obscure village it grew to become the thirteenth richest town in England by 1500, and one of the men responsible for its success was Thomas Spryng III. He was known as the 'rich clothier' and was the most successful of all the clothiers in Lavenham who made the blue serge cloth for which the town became famous. Producing finished cloth was a very labour-intensive business. It took fifteen people – cutters, carders, spinners, weavers, fullers and finishers among them – one week to make a piece of broadcloth 11 metres by 2 metres.

Spryng provided the capital to buy the wool and to set up the mills and looms. At one stage he had 500 people working for him. Hamlets and villages nearby became satellite production centres where weavers worked at their looms and probably managed a smallholding at the same time. Some idea of Thomas Spryng III's commercial empire can be gained from his will in which he named 130 places in three counties where his workers and tenants were to receive a legacy of £100.

Lavenham's church also benefited from Spryng's benefactions. You cannot fail to see it. The church tower is 43 metres high. Built on a hilltop at the end of the High Street, it can be seen halfway across the county and might have been taller, the story goes, if a mason had not fallen off the top during construction. Lavenham's Lord of the Manor, John

Left: The Guildhall, Lavenham, one of two fifteenth-century guildhalls in a town that, by 1500, was the thirteenth richest in England.

Right: Lavenham's Parish Church. Rebuilt in 1485, its size and lavish interior reflect the wealth of the town's medieval cloth industry.

de Vere, suggested that the rich clothiers should join with him in the very expensive enterprise of rebuilding the church in 1485, the year of the Battle of Bosworth in the Wars of the Roses. De Vere, the thirteenth Earl of Oxford, had been Henry Tudor's Captain General and had engineered the victory that ended with King Richard III being dismounted and slain and the Tudors taking the English crown.

Perhaps by way of celebration, Lavenham's businessmen were encouraged to put up the money for this proud-looking church with its splendid tower and its gracious perpendicular windows that flood the nave with sunlight. The interior is full of memorials to the charity of men who made East Anglia a medieval El Dorado.

De Vere and Spryng, who were the main benefactors of Lavenham's church, seem to have vied for space to plaster their arms around the building. The earl paid for the porch, while Spryng built the delightful Lady Chapel. Standing by the porch you can see Spryng merchant marks and de Vere emblems at the base of the enormously expensive tower and, in a final flourish at the very top, the Spryng coat of arms is emblazoned along the parapet no fewer than thirty-two times.

troughs of water mixed with fuller's earth in order to thicken and felt the cloth. Water mills, the clothiers found, could be fitted with mechanical hammers. Rural sites with good streams began to attract the cloth-makers, and by the end of the fourteenth century towns such as Oxford, Lincoln, Northampton and York, where fulling was still done in the traditional way, were showing signs of decline.

On a 'green-field' site England's first capitalists were not only able to escape the bustle of the town but also the restrictive regulations of the guilds that controlled the quality of the product, its price and the workers' conditions of employment. Rural industry in the fifteenth century was in some ways a predecessor of the later Industrial Revolution. Conveniently sited near the raw material, which was to be found on expanded peasant farms, the acres of the gentry and among the large monastic flocks, many villages mushroomed into industrial centres. Lavenham in Suffolk remains almost unchanged as an outstanding example.

The wealthy Spryng and de Vere families of Lavenham were not unusual in the way they contributed to the Church. Other rich families in the Middle Ages set up grammar schools, enlarged Oxford and Cambridge colleges, and founded monasteries, almshouses and hospitals all over the country. It was an astonishingly generous period for charitable giving, and thousands of privately funded institutions began life in this way. Most of them were swept away by Henry VIII in the sixteenth-century Reformation, but one medieval hospital did survive – St Cross at Winchester in Hampshire – and it carries on today according to its founder's charter.

Hospital of St Cross

Jonathan Riley-Smith and I knocked on the door of the porter's lodge at the gate of the Hospital of St Cross and Almshouse of Noble Poverty. Like travellers of some 850 years ago we knew that we could claim the 'Wayfarer's Dole' – food and drink – which the hospital's twelfth-century founder said should be given to the poor. Today, the porter produces a small beaker of beer from a plastic bottle and a slice of bread. It was only a gesture, he explained, a link with tradition. The dole is limited to one gallon of beer and two loaves of bread a day so determined wayfarers need to arrive early – before the coach parties! The porter, wearing a broad, silver cross on his lapel, then opened the gate on a remarkable medieval survival: a large quadrangle complete with a late Norman church, a common room and library, a range of apartments for the 'noble poor' and a beautiful medieval hall.

St Cross was established in 1136 so that 'thirteen poor men, feeble and so reduced in strength that they can scarcely, or not at all, support themselves without other aid, shall remain in the hospital constantly'. The charter also provided for 100 non-residents to receive one square meal a day in a room by the gate, and the beaker and beer and slice of bread offered to visitors today continues that tradition.

Inside the Norman church of St Cross, rows of drum columns, reminiscent of those in Durham Cathedral, support a vaulted ceiling. The earliest part of the church, the chancel, was started in 1160 and the rest grew into its present form over the following two centuries. The architectural mixture

Jonathan and myself receiving our 'Wayfarer's Dole' from the porter at the Hospital of St Cross.

of pure Romanesque and Early English Gothic is very agreeable. But the spacious quadrangle with the 'chapel' in one corner did not evolve into its present form until the middle of the fifteenth century.

Cardinal Beaufort, one of John of Gaunt and Catherine Swyneford's sons, refounded the hospital in 1446 with the support of his half-brother, King Henry IV. Money was provided to look after eight 'noble poor' brothers, but the cardinal also left his mark on the finely carved Beaufort Tower and the range of apartments that make up one side of the square. Attended by the master of St Cross, a steward, several clerks, cooks, bakers, brewers and

Henry VIII and the Dissolution of the Monasteries

Other institutions did not escape so lightly after Henry VIII acquired Parliamentary approval for the dissolution of the monasteries. But the genesis of the king's actions lay, not in the Reformation, but in his tangled marital affairs.

Henry, the younger son of Henry VII, had succeeded his father because of his brother Arthur's premature death. Henry not only gained the throne but also Arthur's attractive widow, Catherine of Aragon, whom he married on becoming king in 1509. It seemed a good match, as royal marriages go, but disenchantment set in

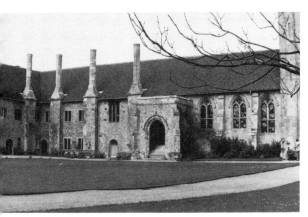

The medieval hospital of St Cross, Winchester. Established in 1136, it is England's oldest charitable institution.

Beaufort Tower, the hospital's fifteenth-century main gate, built by Cardinal Beaufort.

assorted servants, the poor brothers spent their days at masses in the 'chapel' and eating in the late fourteenth-century hall. It is another fine building: a monumental Romanesque doorway leads you into a room 15 metres by 8 with a dais for the high table and a minstrels' gallery at one end.

Today's visitors find that the brethren of the 'Noble Poor Foundation' wear claret-coloured caps and gowns, while the seventeen 'Black Brothers' of Bishop Blois's original foundation favour black caps and gowns. When a brother dies another medieval tradition is observed: the inner door of the Beaufort Tower is closed and the brother's silver cross is placed upon a red cushion and laid on the coffin. Just before the burial the cross is taken off and later fastened by the master to the gown of the next brother to join the community.

Walking into this peaceful and well-ordered fragment of medieval England leaves you wondering how it managed to survive the Reformation and Henry VIII's dissolution. It certainly came under close scrutiny from the king's Visitor General, Thomas Cromwell, who closed down religious houses as quickly as he could compute the value of the lead on the roofs. At St Cross in 1535 he was content to insist on certain reforms: 'the hundred poor shall not be served at the gates as mendicants, like as was long ago accustomed to be done; and such dinners shall be distributed to them who study and labour with all their strength at handiwork to obtain food; and in no case shall such alms be afforded to strong, robust and indolent mendicants, like so many that wander about such places who ought to be driven away with staves, as drones and useless burdens upon the earth.'

when Catherine, after many years, failed to produce a male heir. Henry concluded that a divine blight had befallen his marriage because he had ignored Old Testament teaching and married his brother's wife. Besides, Anne Boleyn had already taken his eye. A papal annulment of the marriage on the grounds of consanguinity was sought but refused. Furious, the king usurped the Pope as head of the Church in England, secretly married Anne, and arranged his own divorce with parliament's approval.

Henry's move against Rome was not altogether unpopular. Reformation was in the air. Martin Luther had signalled its start when he nailed his ninety-five theses (against the Church raising money by the sale of indulgences to build St Peter's in Rome) to the church door in Wittenburg in 1517, almost twenty years earlier. In England the movement to reform some aspects of the Church was particularly strong in the universities and the Inns of Court. But it was the king's desire for money, not for reform, that was the main motive for his attack on the monasteries. The recurring war with France and the king's lavish lifestyle had left his coffers all but empty, and the monasteries proved an easy target. By March 1540, with the surrender of Waltham Abbey, monastic life in England had ended and, with it, centuries of English tradition.

Henry VIII, from a portrait in the Barber-Surgeons' Hall, London.

Monastic tradition cut no ice with Henry VIII's commissioners who were charged with the task of winding up the monasteries. They arrived at Glastonbury Abbey in September 1539 and called on the abbot at Sharpham Park, one of his country manors on the abbey estate. Richard

Glastonbury Abbey

Almost the first thing you see on a visit to the ruins of Glastonbury Abbey is a thorn tree. Its origins, according to a strong Glastonbury tradition, go back to a visit by Joseph of Arimathea, who provided Jesus's tomb after the crucifixion. He is supposed to have travelled to Britain with twelve followers some time in the first century AD, to have made his way along the Cornish and Devon coasts, and established a church at Glastonbury. The thorn tree, near the site of that first church, is said to have sprouted from Joseph's staff. Ever since, it has blossomed every Christmas and Easter. Joseph is also credited by medieval writers as being the bearer to England of the chalice used by Jesus at the last supper – the elusive Holy Grail which King Arthur's Knights of the Round Table had searched for in vain.

William of Malmesbury was convinced that St Patrick was buried in the monastery's tightly packed cemetery, and there is a record of King Canute visiting the graves of the Saxon kings, Edgar, Edmund and Edmund Ironside. Some masonry from a seventh-century church has been found 2 metres under the existing medieval ruins and we know that by the tenth century, when St Dunstan was Abbot, Glastonbury was considered very special.

You get a glimpse of Glastonbury's sixteenth-century grandeur in the nave of the abbey church. Some of the walls still stand to a good height, including two piers of the tower, and there are footings and fragments of walls that mark out the church's extraordinary 200-metre length. The Edgar Chapel survives only in outline at the eastern end of the church, and no more than fragments of the cloister remain. The Lady Chapel, however, is particularly fine. All of its walls survive, along with a carved Romanesque doorway and windows. William of Malmesbury commented that its altar was 'crammed' with the remains of saints so that it was known as the 'heavenly sanctuary on earth'. William also recorded that King Arthur and Queen Guinevere's graves had been identified in the

Glastonbury Abbey, Somerset, England's richest medieval monastery which was suppressed by Henry VIII in 1539. The ruins of the abbey church. The notice (centre) marks the traditional place of King Arthur's grave.

The abbot's kitchen (left) is one of the few medieval kitchens to have survived in England.

monastery cemetery and that in 1278 King Edward I and Queen Eleanor had been present when the graves were opened and the remains reinterred in the choir of the great church. The marble tomb survived until the dissolution, and the site is now marked by a sturdy iron sign.

Whiting, like most of the abbots and priors across the country, had accepted the king as head of the Church and had not openly opposed the divorce. The commissioners reported that they went through the old man's study 'and found a book against the king's divorce . . . and divers pardons, copies of bulls and the counterfeit life of Thomas Becket in print; but could not find any letter that was material'.

Possession of the book was enough in itself. Richard Whiting was imprisoned in the Tower. A search of the abbey revealed 'money and plate hid in the wall, vaults and other secret places'. Accused of theft, the abbot was tried at Glastonbury, found guilty, strapped to a hurdle and dragged through the town to the top of the hill that overlooks the abbey – Tor Hill. Two of his monks, described by the commissioners as 'monkeys', also faced the executioner, and on 16 November 1539 they all lost their heads.

Most encounters with Henry's commissioners did not end up in violence of this kind. Just three other abbots were executed for treason, but all were bullied and threatened until they agreed to surrender their monasteries to the king. Most monks received something in the way of a pension and many abbots and priors ended up as country gentlemen on modest estates. Some monastic churches, such as Tewkesbury in Gloucestershire, were bought from the king for use by the parish (some as schools), and some became cathedral churches with the monks newly employed as the dean and chapter.

The loss, in terms of manuscripts and works of art, was stunning. A whole layer of English culture and learning that had played such a familiar and leading part in the life of the country for nine centuries had been wiped out in only four years. Theologians, however, were still at work in the universities of Oxford and Cambridge.

Queens' College, Cambridge

The 'Erasmus Tower' is a point of reference for any guided tour of the college. It stands proud of the building in a corner of the sixteenth-century court and is where Erasmus, the college's most famous Renaissance don, had his rooms – not exactly in ivory isolation but on the floors below the tower. In the early part of the sixteenth century Erasmus was a leading figure among those academics inspired by the Italian Renaissance. Their 'humanist' (not connected with today's humanists) approach to education placed an emphasis on classical studies, poetry, history, grammar, rhetoric and moral philosophy. Although not necessarily Protestant – Erasmus himself remained a Catholic – they also stood for changes in the Church and by the time Henry VIII, for his own reasons, broke with Rome, the dons at Queens' were among England's most enthusiastic reformers.

They had already welcomed the first printed Bible in 1525. Along with continental reformers, many of them also questioned the Roman Catholic belief in transubstantiation (the physical change of bread and wine into the actual flesh and blood of Christ at the point of communion). In the 1530s, they gave their support to Henry's new directives to the clergy. These included the orders to defend the king's role as head of the Church in England, to abandon pilgrimages, to teach the Lord's prayer, to prohibit the burning of candles for the saints and the souls of the dead, to provide a Bible in English in all churches and to strip them clean of objects of superstitious veneration.

Tangible evidence of these troubled times can still be found in Queens' College library. The original fifteenth-century bookcases have sloping shelves where manuscripts and early printed works were chained to an iron bar. On many of the leather-bound volumes, you can still see where the chain was once attached. A mass book, printed in 1529 and used by the college priests, has a note on the first page that reads, 'the names of Becket and the Pope have been expunged in this copy'. And on the calendar of feast days in the book someone has

Erasmus, one of the major figures of the Renaissance and a don at Queens' College.

The Erasmus Tower, Queens' College, Cambridge. The college was founded by Andrew Docket in 1446, refounded in 1448 by Queen Margaret of Anjou (Henry VI's wife) and founded again in the 1460s by Edward IV's queen, Elizabeth Woodville.

drawn a line right through the entry of 29 December – Becket's feast day. The names of the popes who were also saints were crossed out, and masses for them were no longer said on those days.

Reformers who used Queens' College library, although it was a privileged institution, had to be careful during the turbulent years of Henry's reforms. Paradoxically, the king never embraced Protestant theology and had no hesitation about arresting reformers who went too far. Twenty-five Cambridge men were martyred as heretics in the 1530s and Thomas Cromwell, the 'hammer of the monks', who had masterminded the dissolution of the monasteries, himself lost his head in 1540.

Between 1547 and 1553 Protestant England marched ahead under Edward VI, Henry's son by his third wife, Jane Seymour. Thomas Cranmer, appointed Archbishop of Canterbury by Henry VIII in 1533 and who had begun

Thomas Cranmer 1489–1556,
a portrait by G. Flicke, 1546.

reforms of the prayer book, continued in his post. But the Protestant court was dismissed when the sickly young boy-king died, to be succeeded by Mary Tudor, Henry's daughter by the divorced Catherine of Aragon. Staunchly Catholic, she repealed the Protestant legislation, married the heir to the Spanish throne, returned the English Church to the Pope and the country to Catholicism. Some 300 Protestants were martyred, including Cranmer. Compared with the burning of Protestants on the continent, Mary's record of persecution was mild, but for centuries the martyrs were remembered. They were included in *Foxe's Book of Martyrs*, published in 1560, which was ordered by the Protestant Queen Elizabeth to take its place alongside the Bible in every church in the kingdom.

The Elizabethan Age

The reformers kept their heads down under Mary and served the Catholic queen until 1558 when the country took another direction. Mary's half-sister Elizabeth, Henry VIII's daughter by the Protestant Anne Boleyn, became queen. Out went the altars and the candles of the Roman Catholics and back came the whitewash and the patriotic sermons of the Protestants. Now, the Roman Catholics were on the defensive again.

There had been those who accused Cranmer of sailing with the prevailing wind. It was certainly true of court officials, and the same corps of civil servants and advisers – the reformers who had survived the five-year return to Catholicism – was on hand to guide and implement the new Elizabethan policy. Among them were cool-headed professionals like Thomas Smith who had used the library at Queens' College when he was a fellow there during Henry VIII's reign. Henry had made him the first Regius Professor of Roman Law, and in government service with Edward VI he was showered with honours. Under the Catholic Mary, Smith's advice had still been sought at court, and when a Protestant queen took her place Smith popped up as a commissioner planning the new prayer book, as secretary to Queen Elizabeth and ambassador to France. On his death, Thomas Smith left his books to Queens' College and the pages of his notebooks are full of doodles. One page shows him practising his new signature as ambassador.

The main beneficiaries of the dissolution of the monasteries were the laity. Only seven years after the last religious house had surrendered its treasures and lands, about two-thirds of the seized estates had either been sold or given away by Henry VIII. William Herbert was one of those at court who benefited. He married the younger sister of Catherine Parr, Henry VIII's sixth wife, and was showered with gifts, including a famous nunnery, which is said to have been founded by Alfred the Great, at Wilton on the edge of Salisbury Plain.

Wilton House

Sir William Herbert, first earl of Pembroke, made great improvements at Wilton which became a popular house with successive monarchs, beginning with Queen Elizabeth, who is said to have been both merry and pleasant during her stay in 1574. The first folio of Shakespeare's plays was dedicated to the third earl and his brother, Philip, the fourth earl, and there is a strong tradition that *Love's Labour's Lost* was first performed at Wilton.

A disastrous fire in 1647 meant almost starting again on the house 'with the advice of Inigo Jones; but he being very old', according to the antiquarian John Aubrey, 'could not be there in person and left it to Mr (John) Webb'. Their work has survived later 'improvements' and can be seen today in the imposing south front – a three-storey wing containing Wilton's famous range of state rooms. Altogether, Wilton is a stunning example of English Renaissance architecture. Although in his mid-seventies at the time, Inigo Jones's touch clearly prevails in the two chambers known as the Single- and Double-Cube Rooms. With a predominantly

Above: *The Double-Cube Room, Wilton House. Designed by Inigo Jones in 1649, it was one of the most famous rooms in seventeenth-century England.*

white and gold colour scheme, both are sumptuously carved and painted; great white marble chimneypieces flanked by classical sculptures and ornate doors on whose pediments sculptured figures indolently recline. These rooms have a classical and baroque affluence that rival any seventeenth-century decoration in France.

First owned by Sir William Herbert (right) Wilton House, Wiltshire, became the seat of the Earl of Pembroke. The south front of the house was re-designed by Inigo Jones in the seventeenth century with additions by James Wyatt.

Almost overnight, William Herbert became a great landed magnate with his extensive monastic estate. But the effect of the redistribution of monastic lands went further.

Between the dissolution of the monasteries and the late seventeenth century the gentry in England almost doubled their holdings of land. Gentry families proliferated. We know that they trebled in number in Essex. In Somerset the records show that they quadrupled, and it is hardly surprising that they remained loyal to the system that had made their advancement possible. What is perhaps just as remarkable is that the bulk of the population at the beginning of Elizabeth's reign was still Roman Catholic, yet they were turned around to Protestantism in the remarkably short space of about forty years.

How was it done? Historians believe that it was mostly due to the firmness of Elizabethan government and the people's response to it. Just a year after Elizabeth came to the throne, in 1559, the bishops, most of whom were Catholic, resigned, to be replaced by Protestants. The clergy were obliged to preach against superstition, images, relics, miracles and papal supremacy. Unlicensed preaching was banned. Once more every church had to have a copy of the Bible in English and Erasmus's book of paraphrases. Clergy could marry once again, although they needed the permission of their bishop. They were ordered to dress appropriately, and everyone, on pain of a fine, had to attend church. Most English people reacted then as they would today. They conformed. The government, with a deft touch, did not rigorously enforce the law, and as long as people showed up at church from time to time the authorities turned a blind eye.

One casualty of this period was the coffers of the Church. Whereas, at the beginning of the six-

teenth century, Christians had given lavishly to the Church – over £80 000 had been given in the first decade of the sixteenth century – by the end of Elizabeth's reign churches were receiving very little. Between 1590 and 1600 parishioners donated under £2000. Overall, the level of charitable giving during the Elizabethan age was almost halved. Paradoxically, this cash crisis for the Church as a whole is the reason England still has so many beautiful medieval churches. There was no money to alter them, according to the prevailing fashion, for about three centuries.

The English did, of course, come round to accepting their new Protestant church and one important factor was the emergence of patriotism. We first noticed it in Canterbury, with the tomb of Thomas Becket, but really it was an Eliz-

The classroom at Stratford upon Avon Grammar School. It is highly likely that Shakespeare attended there.

abethan phenomenon – nurtured first by Henry VIII, who liked to be portrayed as a patriot king – released in a stream of xenophobia as the press, controlled by the Elizabethan government poured out tracts, books and ballads depicting Englishmen as God's chosen people. Released from the Latin liturgy of the Catholic Church, preachers delivered patriotic sermons, and when Catholic Spain turned against England, culminating in the challenge of the Spanish Armada in 1588, the country rallied behind 'Gloriana'.

Elizabeth ruled an England that had become self-confident and expansionist in its outlook. Merchants sent their ships into the eastern Mediterranean to establish a lucrative trade with the Levant; privateers like Walter Raleigh and John Hawkins challenged the Spanish and Portuguese empires overseas; the first colonies in North America were established and England's greatest Elizabethan sea-dog, Francis Drake, circumnavigated the world in the *Golden Hind*. And, as the Elizabethan era closed, the formation of the East India Company presaged the glittering prize of an Indian empire.

All this sixteenth-century energy and enterprise was underpinned by Tudor education. And love of learning contributed to the flowering of the English language that found such powerful and subtle expression in Elizabethan literature and drama. Today, Prince Charles cites Cranmer's English, as expressed in his liturgies, as an example of the power of the English language. Tudor education policy required that every parish should have a school, every town a grammar school and every university an ample endowment. Shakespeare must have been a product of the grammar school at Stratford, although sadly the records for that period have not survived.

As to William's religious sympathies, research into his father's affairs has led scholars to believe that John Shakespeare remained a Catholic all his life. But whatever the young William believed, it does not alter the fact that he was able to express his genius because of the education he received. It is sometimes said that his plays are so sophisticated and politically aware that they could not have been written by a lad from Warwickshire with a local education. That simply shows our ignorance of the revolution in education and language that had taken place. Shakespeare was a product of the Tudor education system, which itself stemmed directly from the Protestant belief in the Word, and in the preaching of the Word in church – in English.

The language, so honed and refined by Shakespeare's time that it had become one of the most useful and elegant in Europe, gave expression not only to the theatre and literature, but to a new Protestant Church to which the majority of Englishmen had turned over a period of only forty years. But by the middle of the seventeenth century, England, like the rest of Europe, would be plunged into religious and civil strife.

CHAPTER SEVEN

Cavaliers and Roundheads

*I*n its beauty and form, seventeenth-century English is unsurpassed. It is the English not only of Shakespeare and his contemporaries in the world of literature, but also of the Bible. Jonathan Riley-Smith went so far as to assert that in those days it seemed almost impossible to write a bad sentence in English. Together we were poring over a first edition of the Authorised Version of the Bible of 1611, kept in the library of Lambeth Palace, the home of the Archbishops of Canterbury since the thirteenth century.

'In the beginning, God created the heaven and the earth. And the earth was without form, and void: and darkness was upon the face of the deep. And the spirit of God moved upon the face of the waters.' These two sentences are the first in the book of Genesis, the first book of the Bible, incised into the culture of England. But if education and the English language continued to develop untrammelled, politically Elizabeth's reign was a hard act to follow.

King James and the New Bible

The crown fell to the scholarly and autocratic king of the Scots, James VI of Scotland. The first of the Stuarts, he lacked the common touch of the Tudors and was perceived as remote, partial to the company of good-looking young men, and a heavy drinker. Nevertheless, he arrived as James I of England in 1603 with a store of credit. His religious background helped. The Catholic gentry remembered that his mother, Mary

Lambeth Palace

Lambeth Palace, London home of the Archbishops of Canterbury since the thirteenth century. The imposing Tudor gatehouse was built in the 1490s.

Drafts and redrafts of King James's new Bible translation must have gone in and out of Lambeth Palace daily during the hectic years leading up to its publication in 1611. The imposing Tudor gatehouse still guards the palace's complex of buildings, which small groups of people can visit by appointment. The crypt of the chapel is perhaps the oldest, where a central row of columns with carved capitals, and a vaulted ceiling suggest a date of about 1200. But the chapel itself suffered badly during World War II and it had to be rebuilt in 1955.

The Archbishop of Canterbury's offices and apartments occupy the nineteenth-century wing, which was designed with a breath of Tudor inspiration. However, the Great Hall, gutted during

Lambeth Palace library, housed in the Great Hall where the magnificent hammer-beam roof was rebuilt in 1663.

The Authorised Version's great, leather-bound bulk, designed for use on a lectern, found its way into all of England's seventeenth-century churches. Preachers, opening their sermons, would turn the pages for quotations and gradually the book's majestic language seeped into people's consciousness and, like Shakespeare, has remained a rich ingredient of the English language.

Our conversation and literature are still flecked with echoes of the Bible as we talk about 'casting our bread upon the waters'. We remind ourselves that 'man does not live by bread alone'; and protest that 'the spirit indeed is willing, but the flesh is weak'. The sheer beauty of that seventeenth-century English has a lineage that stretches back to Alfred the Great and his establishment of English alongside Latin as a language of learning. Then for three centuries after the Norman invasion, English was driven underground to languish in the villages and servants' halls until it re-emerged, vibrant and expressive, in Chaucer's epic works of the fourteenth century.

the Civil War by Cromwell's followers, is more Stuart than medieval. Since the seventeenth century it has contained the palace library and even on a busy day the atmosphere is hushed as voices are lost in the intricate woodwork of the magnificent hammer-beam roof high above.

Among the medieval manuscripts collected by Archbishop Bancroft are literary treasures such as the letters of Francis Bacon; Edward VI's Latin grammar book; Elizabeth I's prayer book; six of Caxton's early printed works, and a first edition of King James's Bible. One fascinating item of Stuart memorabilia (right) is a pair of gloves displayed in a glass case in the library. They were reputedly given to Bishop Juxon by Charles I on the scaffold.

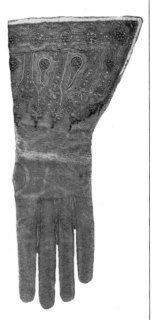

Queen of Scots, had been martyred for her Catholic faith by Elizabeth. Equally, the various Puritan groups were encouraged by the king's Scottish Presbyterian upbringing.

However, Puritan hopes for a full reformation and a complete break with the past were soon dashed. The king would not abolish bishops and so clear away all vestiges of the old Church. Instead, he stood solidly behind the established Elizabethan approach and, lest anyone should misunderstand his position, he clearly intended to be tough on Catholicism as well. Priests were banished and fines were imposed on anyone who did not attend Church of England services – a crackdown provoked a small group of gentry to embark on the notorious Gunpowder Plot. In 1605, the explosives were in place beneath the Houses of Parliament, but before the fuse could be lit an informer tipped off the government and the conspirators, including Guy Fawkes, were hunted down and executed.

This act of treason stirred up anti-Catholic sentiments once more. The Puritans saw popish plots everywhere, and they continued to push the king to further reforms of the Anglican Church. Even before the Gunpowder Plot the king's advisers felt that one way to placate Puritan anger was to agree to the idea that Dr Reynolds, a Puritan leader, put forward at the 1604 Hampton Court Conference for a new edition of the Bible. The Authorised Version – authorised for reading in churches – was to become the king's lasting contribution to England and the English language. Interestingly, the great book, which continues to sell well even now, was the product of six committees totalling fifty-four university scholars. The work of translation began in 1607, and the first draft was completed in two years. That draft was revised by a small committee in nine months and then its publication supervised by Dr Miles Smith (who wrote the preface) and Bishop Bilson.

King James's subjects, while remaining divided on religious matters, continued to show an interest in the New World. In 1607 Virginia was successfully settled; in 1611 the first English and Scottish settlers were planted in Ulster, and nine years later the Pilgrim Fathers navigated the *Mayflower* across the Atlantic to escape religious persecution. Englishmen disapproved, however, at the way the king dealt with England's most dashing seafarer, Sir Walter Raleigh. After the king of Spain complained to James I about Raleigh's attacks on Spanish settlements, the Elizabethan hero was arrested and executed.

Opposition to Charles I

Despite that, the English fascination with exploration and colonisation continued into the next reign, as Charles I succeeded his father in 1625. The new king's attitude to religion was ambivalent. He professed his support for the Protestant Church of England but sought a Catholic wife. Rejected by the Infanta of Spain, Charles married Henrietta Maria of France. Not surprisingly, Protestant opinion was outraged and anxious about the imported popish influence on the new king, who might otherwise have been described as an improvement on his father. Charles was artistic, musical and sexually conventional, but on the debit side he was hopelessly out of touch with the realities of government and the art of politics.

The Church reforms he favoured seemed to many like a return to Catholicism, and his high-handed treatment of Parliament infuriated its members, who blocked his applications for funds to pursue the wars with Spain and France. In 1629, after several years of stormy and bitter encounters, the king decided to govern without Parliament. Members of Parliament, who were drawn mainly from the gentry, went back to their shires angry and worried.

Robert Phelips, for example, was an outspoken critic of royal government. He was Member of Parliament for Somerset. His portrait shows him as a wiry little man with bright-looking eyes. His contemporaries admired his pro-

Sir Robert Phelips, in a portrait dated 1632 and attributed to Hendrik Gerritsz Pots. It can be seen in the hall of Montacute House.

digious memory, and talked about his exuberance of speech. A successful lawyer – he is painted with what looks like a brief in his hand – he was a thorn in the side of the government, opposing the king at every turn while protesting his loyalty to the Crown.

Phelips was on a tightrope. He needed the king's patronage to be a Justice of the Peace and a local bigwig, but to retain his credibility among the Somerset gentry, Phelips had to voice their complaints in Parliament about excessive royal spending and policies that eased discrimination against Catholics. At times, Phelips's balancing act wobbled badly. He was at one time struck off the list of Somerset JPs and on another occasion he was arrested for his outspokenness. A world away from the House of Commons, Sir Robert's country house, Montacute, built by his father in 1601, stands out against the landscape of Somerset like a cliff of honey-coloured stone.

Many of the distinguished Elizabethan and Stuart faces gazing down from portraits in the long gallery at Montacute today would have been known to Robert Phelips, and shared his view of the court – all popery, painting and play acting. But, as Robert Phelips found, to confront the king openly could mean a spell as a prisoner in the Tower. By 1640, after eleven turbulent years of ruling without a parliament, there was very little sympathy left for the king. Even the wealthy merchant classes had been alienated by the dubious ploys the king used to wring more money out of his subjects. The king's government in the 1630s was 'pretty nasty' in the view of historian Dr Christopher Hill. The Archbishop of Canterbury, William Laud, was one of the king's chief advisers and earned himself the hatred of Londoners by 'cutting off the ears of Puritans who were then flogged through the streets on their way to be pilloried'.

The Scots, just as disillusioned as the English, rose against the king after he had tried to impose a new prayer book on the Scottish Presbyterian Church. Eventually, the combination of a kingdom seething with discontent and a financial crisis over military spending meant that the king had to call Parliament.

With the upper hand, Parliament was able to force a package of reforms on the king that greatly reduced his power. Control over the calling and dissolution of Parliament, for example, was to be in the hands of MPs, together with the choice of government ministers and control of the army. Unconstitutional legislation was to be rescinded, the power of the bishops to be curtailed and the two most unpopular ministers were to be impeached and executed.

At about the same time, Ireland rebelled against Protestant rule. It is said that some 30 000 English and Scottish settlers were massacred in

Montacute House

The E-shaped east front of Montacute House rises to three storeys which feature row upon row of elegant tall windows that flood the house with light. As a building it is a bold statement of Elizabethan confidence and success. Unlike its medieval predecessors, the house is beautifully symmetrical. The façade is a miniature sculpture gallery with tall figures of heroic characters such as Julius Caesar, King Arthur and Hector, all striking poses between the windows right across the top of the house. Poetic is perhaps not too loose a word to describe Montacute as you stand in the symmetrical courtyard that features two bow-windowed pavilions on either side of ceremonial iron gates that open into the park.

An inventory of 1630 mentioned Turkish carpets and chairs fringed with gold and lace. The gold and silver plate alone was valued at £470. It was clearly a good life for Phelips at a time when a labourer earned between nine and fifteen pounds a year. Most of the rooms have carved panelling and neo-classical marble fireplaces with carved chimneypieces that reach right up to the ceiling. The plasterwork of chunky geometric design in the library is particularly striking; in this spacious first-floor room the family staged masques and musical evenings.

In the hall you can see how the English country house was changing. At Stokesay Castle, built about

1300, the hall was still the social centre of the house notwithstanding the lord's cosy solar to which the family retreated. Three centuries on, the hall at Montacute had shrunk to the size of a large dining

October 1641, but when the king sought money to take an army to Ireland the Commons refused. MPs were fearful that the king might later use arms against them. As a result the king's troops stormed the Commons, but they failed to arrest his most vociferous opponents. With feeling against him running high in London, Charles was forced to leave the capital.

Civil War

Civil war might still have been avoided had the gentry remained united. What happened, though, left no alternative. Many moderate men from the shires, fearing a total breakdown in law and order which would almost inevitably lead to the loss of their property, switched their support to the king. Royalists and Parliamentarians

Left: *Montacute House, Somerset, built in the late sixteenth century by Edward Phelips; a superb example of Elizabethan architecture.*

Right: *A striking feature of the Great Hall at Montacute is its fine Elizabethan stone screen.*

room, and had become the preserve of the servants. Meanwhile, families in continental Europe continued to use the hall for themselves and the servants were excluded.

Seventeenth-century English family life was quite definitely centred on the family's own dining room, parlour and drawing room. There was, however, still room for an amusing gesture on a grand scale in the hall – a relief in plaster across the entire width of the north wall. The scene shows village life, with a henpecked husband being beaten by his wife for not looking after the baby, and a villager being

punished by 'riding the skimmington' – a pole on which the victim was carried around the village while being jeered at and mocked.

The National Trust acquired the house in 1931 when, after generations of decline, the incumbent Phelips was forced to sell up. With the family silver and furnishings dispersed, the Trust has refurbished Montacute in the Elizabethan and Jacobean style, and in the long gallery – the longest of any English country house – the National Portrait Gallery has added a permanent exhibition of sixteenth- and seventeenth-century works.

raised their banners and took up arms. About half of the nobility were in favour of the king, and the big towns, together with the more populous eastern and southern counties, were for parliament. The gentry were split down the middle and families were divided. Robert Phelips's own sons fought on different sides.

In the early stages of the war the king had better military engineers as well as more experienced commanders. His nephew, Prince Rupert of the Rhine, for example, had seen action in continental Europe during the Thirty Years War.

Prince Rupert of the Rhine. The painting in the National Portrait Gallery Collection dates from the early 1640s and is thought to be by Gerard Honthorst.

Newark Castle

Newark in Nottinghamshire was a vitally important royalist stronghold. The town straddled the crossroads of the Great North Road and the Roman Fosse Way. Newark Castle, on the bank of the River Trent, was one of England's most powerful fortresses. To lose Newark would sever communications between the royalist headquarters at Oxford and the king's supporters in the north. War supplies, shipped from Holland via Hull, passed through Newark. And Queen Henrietta Maria herself, who had exchanged the crown jewels for guns in Holland, stayed overnight in Newark on her return to Oxford. Both towns were hastily surrounded by new defences in the continental style: massive, star-shaped bastions that were linked by earthen ditches and ramparts big enough to absorb the shock of cannon bombardment. Oxford, which was completely surrounded by such gun emplacements, spent about £30 000 on its earthworks, to which the university contributed its gold and silver plate. Every able-bodied male was pressed into labouring gangs and any absence attracted a fine of one shilling a day.

Newark's Civil War defences were distinguished by two star-shaped bastions called the King's Sconce and the Queen's Sconce, part of a system of fortresses beyond the line of the town's new rampart and ditch. Virtually nothing remains to be seen of Oxford's defences – only a fragment of the castle survives within Oxford's gaol – but the Queen's Sconce at Newark has fortunately survived.

The Queen's Sconce stands today in a park on the northern edge of the town as a series of grass-covered hillocks rising to 3 or 4 metres in the rough shape of a star.

He and many other royalist officers had fought in the Spanish, French and German imperial armies and their dashing appearance earned them the name Cavaliers. Parliamentary officers, on the other hand, were drawn mainly from the ranks of country gentlemen who had little or no experience of war. Their troops, raw recruits from the towns, with cropped hair, were soon known as Roundheads.

Civil War battles were somewhat amateur affairs at first. They quickly deteriorated into a mêlée of wheeling and dashing cavalry, sup-

Right: *Newark Castle on the Trent, a royalist stronghold in the Civil War and one of England's strongest fortresses.*

Below: *The Queen's Sconce, Newark, a massive star-shaped bastion on the outskirts of the town.*

The Parliamentary army was equipped with artillery which bastions such as the Queen's Sconce at Newark were designed to resist. Some of the big guns had to be dragged by a team of twenty horses or oxen and in archaeological excavations around Newark cannon balls weighing 30 pounds have been unearthed. The 3-metre-long gun that delivered such a shot was known as 'sweet lips' after a famous whore in Hull. But even that gun, although devastating when used against medieval walls, could not reduce the earthen ramparts of the Queen's Sconce. The third and last siege of Newark in 1646, however, was conducted by the combined armies of Scotland and Parliament, and their 14–16 000 men had the muscle to divert Newark's two rivers, which deprived the castle of its water defences. Sappers built tunnels almost up to the edge of the heavily protected bastions and the defenders, already wracked by disease and hunger, were obliged to surrender.

ported by armour-clad pikemen, and troopers with cumbersome matchlock guns that were often more of a danger to themselves than to the other side. There was such a jumble of uniforms worn by both sides that in the field, friend and foe could only be identified by a colour in their

hat band. There were occasions when both armies chose the same password for the day, adding to the confusion. And it was not unusual for seventeenth-century armies to shrink appreciably if they were in the field too long. Volunteers from London, for example, were notorious for melting away with homesickness. Nonetheless, some battles were tragically bloody, such as Marston Moor in Yorkshire in July in 1644, when about 4500 soldiers lost their lives.

The deployment of Parliament's New Model Army one year later gave the Roundheads an unbeatable advantage. It was England's first standing army, and numbered 22 000 men. Each soldier had standard equipment which included, for the first time in any European army, a uniform for the infantry. From June 1645 red coats were regulation issue, to be worn by British soldiers until World War I. A country gentleman from Cambridgeshire, called Oliver Cromwell, had forged the prototype for this new army from his regiment of horse.

Oliver Cromwell, the MP for Cambridge, was forty-five years of age when he attracted the attention of one of Charles I's courtiers, Sir Philip Warwick. Discussing Cromwell, Jonathan Riley-Smith and I could imagine Sir Philip's lip curling with disapproval as he described the MP's clothes as 'a plain cloth suit which seemed to have been made by an ill country tailor; his linen was plain and not very clean . . . his countenance swollen and reddish; his voice sharp and untunable and his eloquence full of fervour'.

Like Samuel Pepys, Oliver Cromwell had been educated at the grammar school at Huntingdon, followed by further studies at Cambridge and at the Inns of Court in London. He enjoyed music; smoked and drank, and, unlike his Roundheads, had the hairstyle of a gentleman. As a young man he had been through a religious conversion and joined a Puritan group that supported the abolition of bishops. When it came to forming his

Principal battles of the Civil War in England 1642–8. Major Civil War Battles in Scotland were at Auldearn (9 May 1645), Alford (2 July 1645), Kilsyth (15 August 1645).

army he approached like-minded officers and men. He was a strict disciplinarian: swearing cost a soldier twelve pence; drunken troopers were forced to sober up in the stocks; and soldiers caught plundering the countryside could be hanged. But Cromwell's faith was also his inspiration and in his army, made up of preacher officers and corporals, the troops could be heard going into battle singing psalms.

They were not completely beyond human frailty. Royalists were able to dine out on the story of the Roundheads who had surprised a group of Cavaliers playing cards. With great presence of mind the gamblers had thrown the stake money out of the window, Cromwell's men had dived after it and the Cavaliers had escaped

X First Civil War 1642-46
✗ Second Civil War 1648
Royalist Victory
Roundhead Victory
INCONCLUSIVE

⊙ Castle, town or house siege
⊗ Opening major battle, first Civil War
⊠ Last engagement, first Civil War

Marston Moor 2 Jul 1644
Tadcaster 6 Dec 1642
Hull ⊙
Preston 17-19 Aug 1648
Adwalton Moor 30 June 1643
Winceby 11 Oct 1643
Rowton Heath 24 Sept 1645
Nantwich 25 Jan 1644
Newark 22 Mar 1644
Hopton Heath 19 Mar 1643
Lichfield 2-4 Mar 1643
EDGEHILL 23 Oct 1642
Naseby 14 Jun 1645
Powick Bridge 23 Sept 1642
COPREDY BRIDGE 29 Jun 1644
ALDBOURNE CHASE 18 Sept 1643
Oxford
Chalgrove Field 18 Jun 1643
Bristol ⊙
Roundway Down 13 Jul 1643
NEWBURY 20 Sept 1643
Basing House 27 Oct 1644
Langport 10 Jul 1645
Cheriton 29 Mar 1644
Torrington 16 Feb 1646
Sherborne Castle
Exeter ⊙
Bradock Down 19 Jan 1643
Lostwithiel 2 Sept 1644

0   60 miles
0   80 km

Charles I
by John Hoskins.

Cromwell, after Samuel
Cooper's portrait, 1656.

by the back door! But that quick wit and flamboyant style could not triumph in the long run. By the spring of 1646, royalist morale had collapsed, and on 27 April the king, with his hair cut short and wearing a false beard, left Oxford and rode to Newark, where on 6 May he gave himself up to the commander of the Scottish army whose forces had now joined those of Parliament. Parliament had won the Civil War. Or so they thought; Charles I was nothing if not a cunning opponent.

The King's Death and Cromwell's Rule

The Scots released the king into the hands of the Parliamentary army in January 1647 for a consideration of £40 000 and negotiations began, on Parliament's terms, for the king to regain his throne. But Charles played a double game. He secretly negotiated with supporters in England and Scotland hoping to rekindle the civil war. Royalist passions were once again ignited, and in the spring of 1648 a Scottish army crossed the border. There were armies raised in South Wales, the north of England, Kent and East Anglia. But Cromwell's army, after a long summer of campaigns, put down the English and Welsh uprisings, and brought the second civil war to an end by defeating the Scots at Preston and Warrington.

The Army, now fully in control of the country, vowed: 'to call Charles, Stuart, that Man of Blood, to an account for that blood he had shed and mischief he had done, to his utmost, against the Lord's cause and the people in these poor nations'. After Parliament had been purged of any royal support, the king was tried for treason and condemned to death. He met his end on the scaffold outside a window of the Banqueting House of his Whitehall Palace on 29 January 1649.

Banqueting House, Whitehall

The last scene of the English Civil War was played out in a building designed by the architect who introduced the classical Palladian style of architecture to England. The Banqueting House is the last remaining part of the old Palace of Whitehall, and was commissioned by James I as a grand salon for state occasions and the staging of masques.

Before he began to transform English architecture, Inigo Jones had made a name for himself as a producer and designer of masques. He had worked with Shakespeare's contemporary, Ben Jonson, who wrote the scripts and songs for the actors, musicians and members of the court who took part in these most elaborate entertainments. Charles, when he became king, commissioned Rubens to paint the oval and oblong panels of the great ceiling in rich and flamboyant scenes that glorified the Stuart dynasty, and it was under this lofty work of art that Charles I walked to his execution.

The king was brought to the royal apartments of the palace on the morning of 3 January 1649. The commissioners, appointed by a tamed parliament to try the king, had found him guilty of being a tyrant, a murderer and an enemy of the people, and had then condemned him to death. English monarchs had been shuffled off the throne before; but never before, in the full blaze of publicity, had a king been brought to trial and publicly executed. Many of those involved were uneasy and the country seemed to be stunned into inaction. No one lifted a finger to help the king as Oliver Cromwell, in the background guiding and cajoling his colleagues, kept the trial on course.

There was to be no last-minute compromise, as many expected, and whenever the commissioners wavered Cromwell bullied them back into line. One such occasion saw the king and his executioner being kept waiting while three army officers, who had been charged with the responsibility of carrying out the execution, wrangled over whether they should sign the death warrant. Colonel Hercules

The Banqueting House, Whitehall. Designed by Inigo Jones for King James I in 1619, it marked a turning point in English architectural development.

Hunks refused and Cromwell's voice could be heard shouting at him. One of the commissioners, who also faltered at signing, claimed that Cromwell took hold of his hand and guided the pen across the paper.

After several hours' delay the king was called. He was escorted through the palace and along the Privy Gallery lined with troops and sightseers to the Banqueting House. Rubens's wonderful ceiling was only dimly visible as the king crossed the boarded-up room to a window in the stairwell annex and on to a scaffold that had been built out over Whitehall. It was a curious company crowded on to that small wooden platform: two officers; several soldiers; two or three shorthand writers to record the king's last words; the Archbishop of Canterbury, and the executioner and his assistant. The last two looked like something out of a tragicomic play. Both were masked and wore coats buttoned up to their necks. Wigs and false beards completed their disguise. The king asked if the execution block could not be higher – it was only about 25 centimetres off the floor and was more like a quartering block used to dismember the bodies of traitors. One of the officers indicated that nothing else was possible.

Few people beyond that small group on the scaffold could have heard the king's last words spoken from notes on a small piece of paper – the speech protesting his innocence which the 'court' had refused to hear after sentence was passed. To the end he rejected the concept of an anointed king sharing the responsibility of government with parliament. Like the medieval monarchs before him, he believed that his kingship was derived directly from God and that 'A subject and a Sovereign are clear cut different things . . . If I had given way to an arbitrary way, for to have all laws changed according to the power of the sword, I needed not to have come here; and therefore I tell you, and I pray God it be not laid to your charge, that I am the martyr of the people.'

The king took off his insignia of the garter and gave it, with the rest of his jewels, to Bishop Juxon. The king's hair was tucked under his cap; he took off his coat and lay on the scaffold with his head on the block. All that the hushed crowd could see above the black drapes around the scaffold was the flash of metal as the axe rose and fell, once.

The Banqueting House continued to serve Cromwell, the new head of state. He styled himself in 1653 'Lord Protector of the Commonwealth of England, Scotland and Ireland and of the Dominions and Territories thereunto belonging'. He received ambassadors under the Rubens ceiling which, being so high, was safely out of the reach of Puritan zealots. By the time of the Restoration in 1660 the building was playing its full role as a great ceremonial chamber of court. It survived the Whitehall Palace fire of 1698 to remain the only usable part of the palace, and for almost two centuries the royal family used it as a chapel. In 1893 Queen Victoria agreed that the Royal United Services Museum should take it over, and it was not until 1964 that the magnificent building was restored to London as a tourist attraction and superb venue for a party.

Cromwell's rule was to last until his death in September 1658, but the last challenge to his supremacy came from within the army he had created. It had been mobilised to deal with Irish Catholics and royalist supporters who had proclaimed Charles's son as king. Some regiments mutinied and refused to go to Ireland, claiming that Cromwell had not been radical enough in his reform of the state. Discontent was most widespread in regiments that subscribed to Leveller ideas. Astonishingly advanced for their time, the Levellers wanted radical reforms that included universal male suffrage, a written constitution, parliaments with fixed terms and the abolition of capital punishment for petty crimes. Cromwell had put down an earlier mutiny in 1647 by the sheer strength of his personality. Two years later, after cross-examining the Leveller leader, 'honest John' Lilburne, he took a tougher line. 'I tell you, you have no other way to deal with the men but to break them or they will break you.'

The main rebel group of about 850 troopers was at Burford in the Cotswolds, about 45 miles from London, and to reach them Cromwell had to ride nonstop with 2000 crack troops. They arrived at the town about midnight. The Levellers had settled down, quite unsuspecting, for the night. Cromwell and General Fairfax sealed off the town, and with remarkably little bloodshed captured 340 prisoners. They were taken to the church at the bottom of the High Street. After five days three of their number were taken into the churchyard and shot, as an example to the others. It broke the mutiny.

In that fusillade of shots in Burford churchyard, Cromwell broke all resistance to his command. The army went to Ireland as planned, led by Cromwell himself, and the ruthlessness of the sieges of Drogheda and Wexford are embedded

Burford Church

'Anthony Sedley, 1649, Prisoner.' These words, like a groan of despair, are scratched in the leaden lip of the Norman font that is as old as Burford parish church itself. Sedley was one of the 340 prisoners who were locked up and left to think on their actions in Burford church for five days while their fate was considered by a court martial.

Like parish churches all over the country Burford had, by 1649, absorbed its share of the history of the English, and it still reflects that story today. Some of its doorways and arches, which may well go back to the time of Bede and Alcuin, have been reused from an earlier Saxon church. Set into the south-west tower there are three sculptured figures which are reminders of pre-Christian Britain, so closely do they resemble the statuary to be found in a pagan Roman temple of the second century. The west entrance, carved and flanked by six pillars in the Norman style, probably has its original iron-studded oak door, a long-lasting memory of how the English rubbed along with their foreign overlords. Burford's town guild built a free standing chapel in the churchyard in 1500, but by the mid-seventeenth century it had been swallowed up by the expansion of the church itself.

Though Cromwell's troops had swamped the church, they were not to blame for the damage to the interior. The eight stone altars, including one to

Burford parish church.

Levellers' Day service, held each May in the churchyard at Burford.

Thomas Becket, had been pulled down during Edward VI's short reign in the previous century. Burford had also felt the heavy hand of royal power during the dissolution of the chantries in 1547. The school that Burford's chantry chapel supported had to close and it was not until 1571 that a new Elizabethan grammar school took its place. That buff-coloured building still stands just across the road from the church.

In 1649 Cromwell added another layer to the heritage of Burford church. After five days of ordeal by court martial and a series of reproachful sermons by Cromwell and other members of the military hierarchy, four men were selected for execution. At the last minute Cromwell was swayed by the penitent behaviour of the Leveller chaplain, whom he pardoned. The other three men were taken out to the churchyard by the firing squad, while the rest of the prisoners were made to climb a spiral staircase to the roof of the church. The fact that the weight of all those men did not bring all the lead and timbers tumbling down is a tribute to the medieval builders.

The roof-top audience could see the long stretch of red-brick wall in the churchyard where the accused were lined up to be shot. First to be executed was Cornet Thompson, then Corporal Perkins. Finally, John Church met his end. According to a Leveller pamphleteer, he 'stretched out his arms and bade the soldiers do their duty, looking them in the face, till they gave fire upon him, without the least kind of fear or terror'.

Memories of those three men are kept alive by a Levellers' Day ceremony held each year in May. After a parade around the town, there is a service in the churchyard. The vicar of Burford preaches a sermon in front of a plaque by the church door that records the names of the executed men. After the service, Leveller admirers attempt to remember the words of the 'Red Flag' and there is an even shakier rendition of the 'Marseillaise'. In the town, distinguished socialist speakers mingle with morris dancers and Civil War enthusiasts dressed as Roundheads, as they recall the Levellers' remarkable idealism that was snuffed out by Cromwell only to re-emerge centuries later.

in Irish history. A substantial part of the population of Ireland perished during Cromwell's brief campaign of retribution.

Lady Anne Clifford and Appleby

While Parliamentary troops ravaged England's oldest colony a remarkable royalist, Lady Anne Clifford, Dowager Countess of Dorset and Countess of Pembroke, left London in July 1649 for her estates in the north of England. For most of her life she had been at the centre of the social whirl of Stuart London. At the old Banqueting House she had danced in the masques dressed in costumes designed by Inigo Jones, and she was related to, or had married into, many of England's oldest aristocratic families.

Her first marriage, to the Earl of Dorset, had made her mistress of Knole in Kent. The Earl died of a 'surfeit of potatoes' – American sweet potatoes that were renowned for their aphrodisiac properties. And when she married Philip Herbert, Earl of Pembroke, in 1630, Wilton House in Wiltshire became her principal residence. She was there when Inigo Jones supervised the rebuilding of the great Elizabethan house and was greatly impressed by the techniques of the architects and builders. But she once confided that 'the marble pillars of Knole in Kent and Wilton in Wiltshire were to her oftentime but the gay arbours of anguish'. Lady Anne's heart was in the wild expanses of the Clifford estates where she had been born. In the middle of the Civil War she inherited from her cousin a string of ruined castles and the ancient title of Hereditary High Sheriff of the County of Westmorland and Lady of the Honour of Skipton-in-Craven. It was the reason she needed for her return. Perhaps to shut out the horrors of the Civil War, or the memories of her miserable marriage to the Earl of Pembroke, she was, at the

Appleby

age of fifty-nine, determined to create a world apart that reflected the values of previous centuries. She is said to have warned Cromwell that if he interfered she would build up her castles as fast as he could pull them down.

Walking around Appleby-in-Westmorland today, talking to people in the shops and pubs, Jonathan Riley-Smith and I discovered that at times it is possible to imagine that Lady Anne is still travelling the streets of the town. People talk of her as if she might at any moment visit the parish church, where she is buried in splendour and which she refurbished. And at the hospital of St Anne which she founded, her coat of arms, linked with those of her two husbands over the entrance, can prick a modern conscience. When electricity was being considered for the hospital instead of candles and lamps, not all the inmates were in favour, in case Lady Anne might not have approved. She would not have approved of her daughter and son-in-law's fine Restoration mansion built in the inner bailey of Appleby Castle. Sadly her descendants, bored with the upkeep of Lady Anne's other medieval castles, used them as a quarry to build the new house.

Lady Anne's resistance to Cromwell's martial law is something in the English character that has been shared by most Englishmen in successive centuries. England, like her European neighbours, had been buffeted by revolution and regicide, and the institutionalised aggression, bigotry and suspicion of religious minorities during the seventeenth century still have echoes in modern society. Lady Anne's dogged determination not to conform is also a character trait which we all recognise today. And in her eccentricity there is an English longing to find solace in a nostalgic return to a 'golden' age.

The Norman keep of Appleby was probably built on the site of a Roman fort that overlooked a ford of the River Eden. Only a Roman well, recently discovered under the castle, remains from that period, but the Norman earthworks and moats surrounding the inner bailey of the castle are well preserved. There is one particularly fine thirteenth-century drum tower that was part of the Norman defences.

Roundheads and Royalist soldiers had wrecked parts of the castle by the time Lady Anne arrived in 1649. It was uninhabitable, like the rest of her castles. What remains today is the result of her restoration, including the partitions in the various levels of the keep. She did the same to all her castles: Brougham, Brough, Barden, Pendragon (home of the father of the legendary King Arthur) and Skipton. And, eschewing the fashions of the

Appleby Castle, Cumbria. The eleventh-century keep was restored to medieval standards by Lady Anne Clifford in the mid-seventeenth century.

Hospital of St Anne, Appleby (right). Built by Lady Anne Clifford (above) in 1653, it still functions as an almshouse for elderly women.

time – other landowners were demolishing medieval castles and replacing them with grand modern mansions – she restored her castles to their medieval grandeur.

She was determined to live in them, all of them, and for the rest of her life, even as an old lady in her eighties, she trundled backwards and forwards across her estates like a medieval monarch, taking up residence in each castle in turn. Everything went with her: the tapestries, the furniture, her bed, all the plate. She travelled in a litter slung between two horses, while her ladies-in-waiting clung to the seats of her coach drawn by six horses. Her women servants were in another coach and the rest of her staff followed on horseback, ambling along with the pack horses and the carts that comprised the 'riding household'. There was no mistaking her caravan. Her tenants and friends were often part of the entourage. Lady Anne insisted on her right to be accompanied by her tenants, so that travelling between castles there might be as many as 300 people on the road and, on her arrival, the tenants would be received one by one by Lady Anne in her room. She gave the men her hand, kissed the women and dismissed them all to their homes.

Some must have objected to living as if in a time warp, as they did to some of the rents paid in kind. One man, a rich clothier called Murgatroyd from Halifax, refused to pay his share of an annual tribute of 800 hens to the castle of Skipton. It was a custom that went back to Norman times and Lady Anne was determined that it should be kept up. Murgatroyd's share was only one hen, but for that she took him to court, won the case, and paid more than £200 in legal expenses. From the roof of Appleby's keep, you can see two churches that Lady Anne rebuilt in the town below, and halfway down the main street that leads to the castle gate there is another institution for which the countess was entirely responsible, the Hospital of St Anne.

Lady Anne's hospital for thirteen frail and elderly women is like a miniature college quad – a two-storey building around a quadrangle that includes a common room and a little chapel for the use of the occupants. Although Parliament had abolished the Anglican liturgy, Lady Anne took no notice. All her castle chapel priests continued with the Anglican rites and no doubt the priest who used this little chapel's seventeenth-century carved pulpit did so as well. Most of the original pews are still in place and in one corner there is a strong-box put there by Lady Anne, when the hospital was opened in 1653, to contain the title-deeds of properties that would sustain her little community. They have done well. Almost 350 years on St Anne's functions much as it did when its founder planned the hospital.

CHAPTER EIGHT

The Birth of Modern England

One of the best views of London is from the tall, graceful windows of an eight-sided room perched high on the south bank of the Thames. Designed by Sir Christopher Wren, the Royal Observatory at Greenwich is now part of the National Maritime Museum, and Jonathan and I had climbed the steep staircase to the Octagonal Room to see for ourselves evidence of how London developed as a city in the seventeenth century. As we looked out, the portraits of the two Stuart kings of the Restoration, Charles II and James II, looked down on us.

Charles II landed at Dover on 26 May 1660. The welcome afforded him by the people of England, enthusiastic and emotional, swept him to the throne on a wave of nostalgia for the monarchy. In an extraordinary reversal of political fortune, Charles was able to name his own terms. Parliament quickly reverted to its traditional role of an advisory body, although it retained the power to approve or reject the king's appeals for money from taxation.

Within a year, Puritan power had collapsed; Cromwell's remains were exhumed and his head impaled on a pike. The other regicides, who had not either died or fled, were put on trial, but in the event only thirteen people were executed. Parliamentary elections in 1661 returned a 'Cavalier' parliament eager to restore the power of the bishops and a Church of England in the Elizabethan mould. Non-conformists, on the other hand, were driven into obdurate opposition by new laws that put them at an educational, political and social disadvantage.

Old customs quickly returned. In the Palace of Whitehall, for example, the mystical quality of monarchy was reinforced by a ceremony known as 'touching for the King's evil' – a healing touch of the royal hands for a form of glandular swelling. The courtier and diarist, John Evelyn, described Charles II sitting in state in the Banqueting House where a royal official 'calls the sick to be brought or led up to the throne who, kneeling, the King strokes their faces or cheeks with both his hands at once; at which instant a chaplain in his formalities, says, "he put his hands upon them, and he healed them"'.

The other famous diarist of the Restoration, Samuel Pepys, gossiped about the king's sexual peccadilloes – Charles had a voracious appetite for women, and fourteen bastards were officially acknowledged! The fun-loving young king started the centuries-long royal connection with racing at Newmarket, and encouraged playwrights and producers in the reopened theatres which Cromwell had closed. The king's love of the theatre gave the diarists of the day something to say about the actress Nell Gwynn! Restoration comedy brought women on to the English stage for the first time, often in male attire, in order, it is said, to reveal their figures to the best advantage. Plays such as Wycherley's *The Country Wife* placed an emphasis on sexual frankness.

Music returned to the restored Anglican Church and, like Louis XIV, Charles kept an orchestra of musicians who played while he dined and danced through the evening. In the royal chapel, Purcell composed for the king and, as theatre-going regained its popularity, the musicians of the royal chapel could be hired to play in orchestra pits. Charles II was a passionate follower of French fashions.

The Royal Observatory

There was a serious side to Charles II, though,

and also to his brother, James, which became evident when they discussed astronomy and navigation. At Greenwich Park, overlooking a broad reach of the Thames, the king founded Britain's oldest scientific institution – the Royal Observatory. There, discoveries about the physical world tumbled over each other as England's amateur scientists laid the foundations for the technology of the next century. Charles II, Evelyn tells us, talked at length with London's gentlemen scientists and, having become their patron, founded the observatory 'to find out the so-much desired longitude of places for the perfecting of navigation'. The problem that Charles addressed was acute. Navigators could fix their position north or south of the equator by observations of the sun, but distances east and west were almost impossible to determine and it was this problem that the first Astronomer Royal, John Flamsteed, was employed to solve.

Flamsteed's experience of the government's miserliness to him as Astronomer Royal illustrates a consistent trait of the character of English government in Jonathan Riley-Smith's opinion. Even the Royal Society, he points out, granted a royal charter by Charles II in 1662, was given little else, while in other European countries similar organisations were endowed with equipment and buildings by royal or wealthy private patrons. And the cultivation of the cult of the amateur is as familiarly English now as it was then, as anyone trying to wring money out of the government for the arts, learning or science knows all too well. 'The rationale of good housekeeping is, in fact, in the perception of history, really no more than bombast,' says Jonathan. 'There is no rationale about it. What lies behind today's government parsimony is tradition.'

Despite royal parsimony, Greenwich thrived intellectually, and the name became synonymous with the science and technology of astronomy and time-keeping. Charles II's ambition was fulfilled in 1767 when the fifth Astronomer Royal, Neville Maskelyne, published a volume of nautical and astronomical tables which, combined with James Hadley's sextant, gave mariners a more reliable way of determining their position on the oceans of the world.

Fears of Popery

Charles's lavish lifestyle and the trade wars with the Dutch ensured that he regularly petitioned Parliament. He was persistently short of money throughout his reign, and what he did receive from Parliament was never enough. One foolhardy ruse he used to raise money was to sign a

The Royal Observatory

The study of science that flowered so profusely under the Stuart kings made the observatory at Greenwich one of the most exciting places in the world of the seventeenth century. Here, to Christopher Wren's attractive building that is still a landmark on the Thames, England's scientists came from their 'laboratories' in the Royal Society to peer at the heavens: Robert Hooke, the inventor of the microscope and of the technique used to build the dome of St Paul's, a man described as one of the greatest inventive geniuses of all time; Isaac Newton (no friend of Hooke's), the first man to explain the force of gravity; Christopher Wren, who doubled as a distinguished mathematician; and Robert Boyle, one of the founders of modern chemistry.

Set in gravel, and running across the courtyard by the gate to the Royal Observatory, is a metal strip that marks the Greenwich meridian. If your eye travels up to the mast at the top of the Observatory, you can see a time-ball which is still dropped at exactly one o'clock every day – a signal installed in 1833 for ships in the Thames to set their chronometers.

Christopher Wren, who had by this time rebuilt

The Royal Observatory, still a landmark for navigators of ships on the Thames, is today a museum that contains some of the world's earliest telescopes and navigational instruments.

PROSPECTUS INTRA CAMERAM STELLATAM.

A contemporary picture of the Octagonal Room with a telescope in use.

most of London's churches after the Great Fire in 1666, had been given a budget of £500 for the building. The money came from the sale of some spoiled naval gunpowder. Bricks were collected from an old fort at Tilbury and some more stone came from a disused gatehouse at the Tower of London. Wren described his building as a new house 'for the observer's habitation and a little for pomp'. The lower floors of the main building now contain the world's most important collection of astronomical and navigational equipment, including John Harrison's famous chronometer. But at the top of the building Jonathan and I stepped into what must have been one of the most elegant rooms in seventeenth-century London. It is a perfect octagon with tall windows overlooking Greenwich Park and the palace started by Inigo Jones for James I's queen, Anne of Denmark and completed for Charles I's Queen Henrietta Maria. On the river bank we could see the enormous grey bulk of Wren's Royal Naval College which was intended to be another royal palace.

The Octagonal Room, restored to its seventeenth-century grandeur by the National Maritime Museum, is clearly the 'little pomp' envisaged by its architect. But as an observatory for John Flamsteed, the building was only a shell. The king had told the astronomer to get on with his observations, but without providing any of the equipment needed. Flamsteed had to buy it all out of his salary of £100 a year. The son of a poor family in Derby, he spent years begging and borrowing scientific equipment for his job. Perhaps it is not surprising that he became obsessive about his results and feared that the gentlemen scientists from the Royal Society would pirate his work. He called Newton 'our great pretender' and 'a robber', and it was years before his catalogue of the heavens – one of the greatest achievements of English science – was published. The Octagonal Room and the little brick observatory alongside, where his first telescope was installed, have little in the way of Flamsteed's original equipment exhibited in the scene which has been recreated for visitors. When he died, in 1719, his widow, perhaps as a final gesture of defiance and bitterness, cleared the place out.

secret treaty with his much wealthier cousin, Louis XIV of France. Charles put his name to a document that agreed to an Anglo-French alliance against the Dutch, and also to a French grant of £300 000 a year for England's war chest. The clause in the treaty that clinched the deal on the French side was Charles's commitment to return England to Catholicism. Whether or not the laid-back and cynical Charles was serious is still debated but, inevitably, details of this remarkable arrangement leaked out. Protestant suspicions, already aroused by the king's toleration for Catholics, flared up across the country.

England was once again wracked by fears of popery, and the Duke of York, Charles's brother James, who had become a Catholic convert in 1669, was forced by Parliament to resign his position as Lord High Admiral. In a conciliatory move that would later be significant, Charles arranged that his brother's daughter, Mary, should marry the Protestant William of Orange. But the country's fears that the court was a hot-bed of Catholicism continued to build up, and a witch-hunt of Catholics was set in train after a defrocked priest proclaimed that a popish plot had been hatched to murder the king.

Parliament by this time had polarised over the succession to the throne. (As things were in 1680, the king's brother, James, was the heir if Charles did not produce a legitimate son.) And it was the question of the succession that produced the first recognisable political parties, known as Tory and Whig. Led by Lord Halifax, the Tories, although staunchly Anglican, wanted no interference with the natural line of succession. They were for the status quo. But Lord Shaftesbury's Whigs took their campaign to the streets of London in an attempt to exclude James's claim to the throne because of his religion. Interestingly, Whig and Tory were the names each party used to taunt the

St Germain-en-Laye

other. Whig meant a sour, bigoted and mean Presbyterian; Tory was a nickname for an Irish, papist bandit. But the country, remembering the horrors of the Civil War, rejected the more strident Whigs and plumped for the party of the king.

Charles suffered a fatal stroke in 1685, but before he died a priest was smuggled into Whitehall Palace to receive him into the Catholic Church. James became the first Catholic king of England since Henry VIII. He quickly put down a rebellion led by Charles's eldest bastard son, the Duke of Monmouth, and set about returning the Church of England, and the English, to the Catholic fold. He probably expected this to happen quite naturally once legal restraints on Catholics were lifted and a more tolerant religious climate was established. Legislation that discriminated against Catholics and non-conformists was repealed, and James promoted Catholics to key posts in the navy, army and the shires.

But James had completely misjudged the country. Far from religious tolerance gaining a hold, people remained fearful of a Catholic takeover. Whig supporters, still the most adamant opposition in Parliament, sent a secret invitation to the Protestant Prince William of Orange in Holland to offer him the throne. William had enough English royal blood to make him acceptable to many people. He was the son of Charles I's daughter and at Charles II's instigation he had, of course, married James II's daughter, Mary. The Whigs' intention was that William and Mary should rule England together.

Seizing an opportunity of a lull in his war with Louis XIV and taking advantage of what the Protestants called a God-given favourable wind, William crossed the English Channel and landed at Torbay in Devon. With him was an army of

James II and his queen, Mary of Modena, were welcomed at St Germain-en-Laye by Louis XIV: 'This is your home; when I come here you will do the honours to me, and I will do so to you when you come to Versailles.' The exiles were lucky. St Germain was every bit a royal palace and had been vacated by Louis only six years earlier when his new palace at Versailles had been completed. The château of St Germain, just outside Paris, still dominates the town as it did when James and his party arrived. It is a vast barracks of a place, four storeys high and built around a five-sided courtyard. Its setting, then as now, is, however, superb. It stands on a plateau above a bend of the Seine and commands a panoramic view of Paris across the valley. There is still enough left of the park in front of the palace to imagine what an idyllic place it must have been in the seventeenth century – surrounded by forest where the exiled king could indulge in one of his favourite pastimes, hunting.

Some of the formal gardens and terraces have survived to be used by townspeople and visitors; and part of the terrace along the escarpment overlooking the Seine, which was once 100 metres wide and over 2 kilometres long, makes a pleasant afternoon walk, as it must have done for James and his courtiers. James's court also had the use of St Germain's famous hanging gardens, complete with grottoes described as the most elaborate in Europe. Very few traces of these remain today.

The château now houses France's national collection of antiquities and the echoing galleries full of objects from prehistory offer only a hint of the rich decoration of the royal apartments on the first floor. Contemporary descriptions talk of gilt-framed mirrors and great silver vases loaded with flowers, columns decorated with gold filigree work, and, adjoining the royal apartments, a theatre built by Louis XIV. There, under a vaulted ceiling decorated with carvings of roses and fleurs-de-lys, Louis XIV acted and danced with his courtiers. Many of Molière's plays, including *Le Bourgeois Gentilhomme*, were first performed in Louis's theatre.

The Château of St Germain-en-Laye, birthplace of Louis XIV and James II's palace of exile after the Glorious Revolution of 1688.

Dutch and exiled Englishmen who marched together on London. This was the English Revolution, though, as modern historians point out, revolution for seventeenth-century English people had more to do with completing a circle rather than simply overturning what had gone before. James II, remembering his father's fate, threw his great seal into the Thames and fled to France.

The New Constitutional Monarchy

James II's son-in-law and daughter then accepted the throne, dismantled discriminative legislation against Protestant dissenters and, in what became known as the Glorious Revolution (though it was not entirely bloodless), introduced a Bill of Rights that gave Parliament for the first time a recognisably modern role. William and Mary became England's first constitutional monarchs and the notion of the divine right of kings, so firmly a part of English kingship for more than a thousand years, began to fade as James II went into exile with his group of Catholic courtiers.

But James II's court in exile had none of that panache and gaiety. It was very devout, rather rigid, somewhat austere, and devoted to the impossible dream of returning in triumph to England. Neither James nor his queen was a good judge of character. The palace seethed with spies and plots against the constitutional monarchs in England, and despite Louis's allowance of 50 000 francs a month, James's court was always poor. He died in 1702 and was buried in the church opposite the main entrance to the château; according to the inscription on his marble memorial in a side chapel, only 'the king's more mobile parts' were reburied there in 1818. What happened to the rest of his remains from the original grave is uncertain. But reading that inscription and looking up at the faded blue and gold decor of the side chapel, with royal coats of arms, lions and dragons and motifs of a 'J' surrounded by crowns, Jonathan Riley-Smith and I found it impossible not to feel a pang of sadness for this exiled king.

Although Jacobite exiles kept the idea of a return to England alive – James himself made one bid for power when he fought King William at the battle of the Boyne – there was little sympathy for the reinstatement of a Stuart monarchy. New trends in political and religious thought also opposed traditional arrangements and made the king's return impossible.

The thinker who contributed most to the development of religious toleration, and later to the success of the new English constitutional monarchy, was John Locke. Born in Somerset in 1630 to a Puritan family, Locke was educated at

Winchester and at Oxford, where he became interested in science and medicine. In 1667 he joined the household of Lord Ashley, who, as the Earl of Shaftesbury, became the leader of the Whig party.

Locke endeared himself to Shaftesbury by supervising a surgical operation that involved lancing a cyst on Shaftesbury's liver. Incredibly, the patient survived and thereafter Locke served his master both in government and opposition. The two men were forced into exile after an abortive attempt by a group of Whigs in 1683 to assassinate King Charles and his brother James on their way back to London from a race meeting. Locke, although probably not involved in the fiasco himself, fled to Holland. There, in Amsterdam, he came under the influence of an intellectual Calvinist sect called the Remonstrants.

John Locke returned from exile in Holland to take up a place as an adviser to the influential people at the centre of England's political life. Working for the new government of William and Mary, Locke reorganised English coinage and formulated economic policy at the newly formed Board of Trade. The Bank of England came into existence in 1694 under John Locke's guidance.

Ironically, though, England was once again ruled by a monarch who was a foreigner – a Dutch Calvinist who regarded the English as an inferior race. Just as it had been for England's medieval kings, French was William's first language. Everything he wrote had to be translated into English, which he spoke imperfectly. A very dry character, sullen with people, boorish in his table manners, he was described by London society as a 'low Dutch bear'. But on the battlefield he was a man to be reckoned with. As Eng-

Remonstrant Church, Amsterdam

The Remonstrant Church in Amsterdam is tucked away behind a row of houses that fronts on to one of Amsterdam's canals. It is almost impossible to find because when it was built the Remonstrants were forbidden to build their churches with a street frontage and the only access is through a narrow alley. This almost secretly located church is a delightful surprise – a large, cube-shaped interior has two tiers of galleries that wrap around three sides of the church, almost giving the impression of a small seventeenth-century theatre. The pillars are painted to look like marble and overhead a barrel-vaulted ceiling is painted blue. The focal point of the church is not the communion table or altar, but the carved pulpit against the back wall where the preacher could be seen from all parts of the church. The word of God was paramount.

Remonstrant Church, Amsterdam. Built in the mid-seventeenth century as part of a seminary, it retains all of its original features.

Interior of the Remonstrant Church before renovation.

A theological seminary was founded here in 1634 and by the time that Locke sought sanctuary in Amsterdam almost fifty years later, Philip Van Limborch was the professor of theology. He was a most impressive teacher and introduced Locke to the aspect of Remonstrant theology that laid emphasis on the individual. Remonstrants believed that it was for each individual to read the scriptures and come to his own conclusion about the faith. This was a theme that had fascinated Locke for the previous twenty-five years and in Amsterdam, under the influence of the Remonstrants, he refined his ideas and produced his famous *Letter on Toleration*.

Writing in Latin to reach the widest possible academic audience, he propounded that it was blasphemy for the state to force a particular version of Christianity down the throats of believers. He saw the Church no longer as a monolithic institution but as a disparate body, made up of religious societies that should be mutually tolerant. Moreover, he wrote that the state had no right to interfere with a man's conscience.

These were explosive ideas in an age of intolerance and absolutism in both Church and state. But, in what may seem curious to the modern mind, Locke's tolerance stopped at atheism and Catholicism. Like most Protestants at that time he believed that the Catholic Church was a seditious organisation and could not be tolerated. Nevertheless, his ideas were way ahead of his time, and among European Protestants he was the most widely read of all seventeenth-century philosophers.

In England, his ideas led to a fundamental debate within the Church of England; an argument between those who believed that the Church of England should be an umbrella giving shelter to a broad, but Anglican, spectrum of belief, and those who believed, like Locke, that all churches had a right to existence. That debate, launched in the Remonstrant Church in Amsterdam, resounded through the forums of the Church of England until the nineteenth century, and was a major factor in shaping the outlook of today's Anglican Church.

The Remonstrants themselves, after long periods of persecution, were recognised as an independent church community in 1795 and were able to build up a large and influential following. A hundred years ago there was a Remonstrant church in just about every town in Holland, but decline in the twentieth century has been almost terminal. The church in Amsterdam was in use until 1954 when dwindling numbers forced a move to a suburb.

Under a thousand elderly people adhered to the church in the 1980s and the empty and beautiful Amsterdam building, attacked by dry rot and general neglect, was used as a rehearsal room by pop groups and choirs. In the late 1980s the Remonstrant community, however, summoned its strength to save the building and over a million pounds is being spent on restoration with the intention that it should be reopened as a concert hall. It will look exactly as it did three centuries ago.

land's last warrior king, he fought the French and effectively dealt with James II's forces on the banks of the River Boyne where Protestant Ulstermen still meet to drink a toast to him.

The West Indies Slave Trade

Religion and politics were not the only pre-occupation of seventeenth-century Englishmen. Trade with England's traditional European markets continued to flourish, and across the Atlantic trade followed the flag in an expanding English empire. But the trade was not only in commodities, it was also in human beings – the slave trade.

It all started innocently enough. English settlers in the West Indies were no different from the hard-working American colonists of the early seventeenth century. A surprisingly large number of them, 30 000, had settled on the English islands of the Caribbean during the reigns of James I and Charles I. They had gone as farmers and artisans to escape from high inflation, low-paid agricultural jobs or religious persecution; or they had left for lack of opportunity at home as the population steadily increased. The Windward Islands had been settled first, beginning with St Christopher (St Kitts) in 1624. Barbados, settled three years later, gave each new arrival a grant of 10 acres plus an additional 10 acres for each indentured English servant.

The new settlers scraped a living from trading cotton and poor-quality tobacco until, in the early 1640s, Dutch merchants introduced the idea of growing sugar. The merchants provided the know-how, the processing equipment and, in the early years, a market in Holland for the sugar. But they also made the whole enterprise possible, and profitable, by supplying a labour force of African slaves. The English islands of the West Indies, beginning with Barbados, were

Royal Fort House, Bristol

Thomas Tyndall could probably have counted his ships in Bristol docks from the windows of his elegant Bath-stone mansion. The Tyndalls were Bristol merchants who had made part of their wealth in the lucrative trade to the West Indies. The house takes its name, Royal Fort House, from the Civil War fort which Prince Rupert had garrisoned for the king in 1643. Only a part of one bastion remains from that Stuart fortress but the house, which is now home to Bristol University's Department of Music, was built partly with profits from sugar and slaves. In the last quarter of the eighteenth century over seventy ships a year cleared the harbour for the direct crossing to the West Indies, while about half as many made the triangular voyage to the west coast of Africa, with baubles, muskets and spirits to trade for slaves. They sailed across to the Caribbean and back to Bristol with sugar, cotton and tobacco.

The interior of Royal Fort House is breathtaking. All the principal rooms are adorned with

transformed in just twenty years. They became islands of wealth. Visitors in the 1660s talked about Barbados as one continuous garden, 'a little England' divided into parishes named after the saints; there were villages such as Speights-

Left: *Royal Fort House. Built in the mid-eighteenth century for Thomas Tyndall, a Bristol merchant who made his wealth in the West Indies trade.*

Right: *Detail of the plasterwork depicting a fox in pursuit of its prey.*

Below: *The hall of Royal Fort House.*

plasterwork and wood-carvings of superb quality. The house was lived in by members of the Tyndall family until 1916, when the university bought it and, recognising its architectural merit, made sure that the delicate plaster and woodwork survived in excellent condition. The staircase, framed by a broad, flat-topped arch, has some of the most eye-catching decor.

Standing proud of the walls are vines modelled in plaster that climb and swirl around the stairwell. Amongst the foliage, the designer, who may have been inspired by eighteenth-century Chinese wallpaper, created a menagerie of plaster woodland creatures: a diminutive fox trying to climb a vine to reach a hen, a caterpillar, a snail, a cow, and a duck chased by a dog.

In the house today, students can often be heard playing eighteenth-century music, which echoes through the building and creates a soothing, civilised background for what must have been one of Bristol's most elegant mansions. But much of the wealth that lay behind it came from an English trade in human beings which historian Richard Dunn believes was 'one of the harshest systems of servitude in western history'.

The door of the music room, framed by an extravagant design carved in wood by a master craftsman.

town and Bridgetown, and a wild hinterland, nostalgically called Scotland.

Not unnaturally, some of this wealth, made possible at least in part by the slave trade, found its way back to England sooner or later. In Bris-tol, for example, merchants grew rich on the business they did in the colonies. The city itself, one of the principal ports for trade with the West, became an architectural monument to its new-found prosperity.

Slaves working a sugar plantation in Antigua.

Jamaica, biggest of the English islands in the Caribbean, had been seized from Spanish colonists in 1655 by a Cromwellian naval expedition. English buccaneers as well as sugar planters were attracted to the island, which became notorious as Captain Morgan's pirate stronghold. But sugar was king on all the English Caribbean islands. There, during the seventeenth century, no fewer than a quarter of a million slaves were landed who had the status of chattels from the moment they arrived.

A brand mark burned into their flesh by a silver branding iron completed the slaves' preparation for bondage which, in most cases, was for life. Some were no more than children when they arrived; most were males between ten and twenty years of age. Death caused by overwork, poor nutrition and disease was high, and the slave traders sailing out of London, Bristol and Liverpool were gainfully employed in topping up their numbers. On some voyages, half of the poor wretches locked below decks might die, and it was only when the price of slaves rose substantially, from three pounds to thirty pounds per head in the late seventeenth century, that the mortality rate on the 'Middle Voyage' fell from about twenty-five per cent to ten per cent.

Henry Whistler, who kept a journal of his travels through the West Indies in 1665, remarked that the gentry on Barbados, 'in one of the richest spots of ground in the world', had a better life than in England. He observed, however, that among the English, Scots, French, Dutch, Irish, Spanish, Jews and native Indians, the 'miserable Negroes' were encouraged to breed as many children from as many wives as they pleased. 'Our English here doth think that a Negro child the first day it is born to be worth five pounds. They cost them nothing in the bringing up, they always go naked. Some planters will have thirty more or less about four to five years old. They sell them one to the other as we do sheep.'

Harsh punishments were meted out for misdemeanours. Dr Hans Sloan, when he visited Jamaica in the late 1680s, mentioned punishments such as castration, rubbing lash wounds with melted wax, lopping off half a slaves' foot with an axe or, for capital crimes, impaling a slave's body with stakes and slowly burning him alive; punishments 'scarce equal to some of their crimes' in Dr Sloan's view.

During the course of the seventeenth century plantations became bigger as smallholders sold out to the big planters and drifted into the towns to become a new class of landless, poor whites. The planters who consolidated their lands and who controlled the islands' assemblies owned hundreds of slaves and displayed their wealth in big houses, carriages and fine clothes that were more suited to the climate of England than the tropics. These men were free-wheeling entrepreneurs with a lavish lifestyle, but as the islands filled up with resentful slaves (by the early eighteenth century the whites were outnumbered four to one), the planters' main ambition was to leave their tropical islands and become absentee proprietors. Many returned to Bristol where they built fine mansions like Thomas Tyndall's Royal Fort House.

Enclosures and the Drift to the Towns

The plantation owners returned to a country with more mouths to feed than it knew how to cope with. The previous century had seen the population surge ahead from about four and a half million to about six million, numbers not known since before the plague of the fourteenth century.

Emigration to the American and Caribbean colonies – about 400 000 in all – had helped to ease the pressure, but throughout the 1700s England's burgeoning population forced profound changes on the country. Agriculture had to be cranked into a higher gear to feed the many more mouths. In the interests of efficiency, medieval strip farming, such as we saw in the huge

open fields at Laxton in Nottinghamshire, was abandoned in favour of smaller fields. Usually, peasants and landowners divided the open fields by agreement in a process that had been going on steadily since about 1500.

'Enclosing' – referring to the hedges and fences which were put in to mark out the field boundaries – gathered pace during the seventeenth century, to the detriment of the poorer peasants who missed out on the profits to be won from more efficient farming. They suffered because the new fields, which could be better drained and planted with new crops and improved pasture, had to be fenced. It was a major item that was beyond the resources of many peasant families and those who could not afford to fence were obliged to sell out to their richer neighbours who could, and they set about changing the English landscape into its familiar patchwork quilt of hedged fields.

Westbury Hill is perhaps best known for its white horse carved into the chalk side of the hill. From there you can look out on mile after mile of fields which maintain their seventeenth-century appearance. In many places in England, you can see where the open fields were enclosed by looking along the curve of hedges; a long hedge was planted along the furrow that had been part of an open field. And on either side of hedges you can often still see the ripple effect of the medieval ridges and furrows under the pasture. There are also fields with scattered lumps and bumps that mark the sites of villages that were enclosed out of existence. Hundreds of villages disappeared like that in the seventeenth and eighteenth centuries.

The modern English landscape pictured from over Westbury Hill in Wiltshire. The patchwork quilt of fields is the result of enclosures during the sixteenth and seventeenth centuries.

It is ironic that while the English planters in the West Indies were importing slaves, a kind of wage-slavery was being created in England among a new landless class that was unique in Europe. Hundreds of thousands of people had been shaken out of subsistence farming into poverty. Very often, the land they once farmed was turned into pasture for sheep, as mutton became popular on English tables. But flocks of sheep provided little work for armies of landless people and where there was work to be done the supply of labour far exceeded demand, so farmers could name their own low wages.

Large numbers of dispossessed peasants migrated to towns and cities, so much so that, by 1700, they were bursting at the seams. London was the most extreme example with a population of about 60 000 in the 1520s. By 1600 that had grown to at least 200 000 and by 1700 there were

A panorama of the City of London by Visscher, published in 1616. Dominating the picture, and somewhat exaggerated in size, is the medieval St Paul's which was rebuilt by Christopher Wren after the Great Fire of London in 1666. St Paul's spire was struck by lightning in 1561 and never replaced. Shakespeare's Globe theatre is shown (left foreground) on the Southwark bank of the Thames and the bear-baiting garden (far left), like the Globe, is flying a flag to signify the start of a performance.

almost 600 000 people crammed into the capital and its suburbs.

The drift to the south-east of England is hardly a recently phenomenon. In the seventeenth century, three-quarters of the population already lived in the south and east, and London had become disproportionately important as the centre of government, law, fashion and fun. It had also become a city of businessmen who, in the seventeenth century, controlled most of England's trade. In the 1660s, London began to rival the role of Amsterdam as an entrepôt for international trade, processing produce from the colonies and re-exporting it to other European countries. At times it must have seemed as if half of England's produce was rumbling along in carts towards London, so voracious was the city's appetite for agricultural products. The result was that agricultural rents soared and, as farmers got better and better prices with buyers competing for what they produced, inflation added another twist in a spiral of misery for the unemployed.

Living conditions in the towns were often dreadful. Houses were divided and subdivided. Gardens were built over to create more accommodation as the towns sucked in people from the countryside. Almost every house in the big towns was infested with rats, and with heaps of rubbish in the streets and fly-blown outdoor privies, gastro-enteritis spread easily and claimed the lives of many children. Recent studies in parish registers of the sixteenth and seventeenth centuries reveal that about a fifth of all children died before they were one year old and, if they survived the bouts of plague that could carry off a third of a town's inhabitants, life expectancy in the seventeenth century was between thirty-two and forty years.

A network of improved roads, all radiating from London, served the migrant English. But from the 1660s onwards, those on foot would have been overtaken by the first stage coaches, as they ferried rich travellers at a cost of a shilling for 5 miles. Improved communications also meant that disease could spread more quickly. Any new and nasty ailment shipped into London – more than half of England's trade was handled by the port of London – could be transmitted throughout England.

In the North Midlands village of Eyam, for example, the plague of 1665 is said to have arrived in a case of clothes. People soon began to die, but the rector persuaded his parishioners not to leave the village and thus spread the disease. They all stayed and eighty per cent of them died, but the outbreak was contained and the annual church service commemorating their courage and self-discipline is still held on the last Sunday in every August. It was not until the Great Fire of 1666 that the recurring bouts of plague subsided. But even in the rebuilt city, smallpox, influenza and particularly tuberculosis caused a large number of deaths each year.

As we have seen, interest in science had begun to grow and applied science had started to blossom as a focus of study. At this time, religion and science went hand in hand and Sir Isaac Newton's theological work, for example, was as well known as his scientific theories. The seventeenth century was also an age of millennial hopes, a time when scientists had tried to predict the time when Christ's kingdom would come on earth. 1651 had been the preferred date. But with the Enlightenment around the corner, science and religion would soon part company, and English women would question their role in a male-dominated society.

As for business and commerce, at the beginning of the eighteenth century a combination of circumstances meant that England not only had expertise as a trading nation and a rich supply of raw materials such as iron ore and coal, but also a head start in technology and a pool of unemployed labour willing to consider any work. Together, they brought about the Industrial Revolution – the first in the world. Workers, such as those from Bratten in Wiltshire, in the shadow of Westbury Hill, may have travelled north, to where the Industrial Revolution first began to take shape, Ironbridge Gorge in Shropshire.

The men and women who prepared the way for the Industrial Revolution in the early 1700s

Ironbridge Gorge

This little valley accounted for about a quarter of all the iron smelted in England by the end of the eighteenth century, and the countryside vibrated with the thud of hammers, the rumble of horse-drawn railway wagons and the roar of the blast furnaces. Eighteenth-century visitors wrote that they could hear the noise of this extraordinary industrial

Above: *The Ironbridge Gorge of the River Severn. Its industrial noise and smoke in the eighteenth century could be heard and seen miles away.*

valley from miles away, and at night the reflected fiery light from the furnaces was a beacon that guided travellers to what some people described as a descent into hell.

Squeezed into the core of a seventeenth-century blast furnace Jonathan and I felt uncomfortable and claustrophobic. The furnace, in a side valley of the Ironbridge Gorge called Coalbrookdale, is a bunker-like construction with a bell-shaped interior. A large water-wheel once drove the bellows that kept the furnace going and above our heads the bricks curved up to a round hole through which the mixed iron ore and fuel were tipped. Getting into this furnace on our hands and knees along a 5-metre-long tunnel meant that we had arrived at, quite literally, the heart of what is perhaps the world's most important industrial monument; the actual blast furnace that gave life to the Industrial Revolution. In appearance, it is not unlike the furnaces that were first introduced into England

Right: *The world's first bridge to be constructed in iron in 1779 still spans the valley where English iron masters proved that cast iron – the Industrial Revolution's equivalent of modern plastic – could be safely used for major civil engineering projects.*

from the Low Countries in the late 1400s – 6 metres square, almost 10 metres high, and with walls up to 2 metres thick.

In themselves, blast furnaces represented a technical innovation that greatly increased the production of iron ore, but they had an insatiable appetite for fuel. One of these monsters turning out 15 tons of iron a week consumed the timber from about one acre of woodland a day. It had been recognised as a problem for over a century. As far back as the 1580s iron masters had been restricted from working in areas on the outskirts of London because of their effect on forests near the capital. Indeed, large parts of the south-east of England were losing their timber to this essential, but destructive industry, and iron masters were obliged to set up in less populated parts of the kingdom. Wood to make charcoal was in such short supply in the seventeenth century that some furnaces had to close down for a time and wrought-iron forges had to import pig iron from as far away as Spain and Sweden to keep going. Coal, of which there was an abundant supply, had been tried, but the impurities it introduced into the iron made it crumbly and useless.

That was the situation that faced Abraham Darby (1667–1717), who settled in Coalbrookdale in the early 1700s. A Quaker, he had been a wire-maker in Bristol and on arrival in Coalbrookdale had leased an old furnace to produce his own iron. In trying to solve the fuel problem, he experimented with coke and found that the local coal, which was low in sulphur, gave similar results to charcoal. When he added limestone, which was also abundant, molten pig iron flowed from the furnace free from impurities. Darby had broken through the obstacle to mass-production of cast iron. Darby's son perfected the process forty years later, and by 1791 Britain had eighty-five coke-fired blast furnaces working twenty-four hours a day.

The banks of the Severn and the side valleys of Ironbridge Gorge became a microcosm of eighteenth- and nineteenth-century British industry:

Abraham Darby's iron smelter in which he successfully experimented with coke as a fuel in 1709. Over the entrance, the date of 1638 records the first furnace. It was rebuilt in 1777 to cope with the production of the 370 ton of iron needed for the first iron bridge. The furnace, which was last used in 1815, has been conserved on its original site and is protected by a glass and wood pavilion.

coal mining; ore extraction; smelting; iron working; canal-barge building at the little port established at the Severn end of the Shropshire Canal; tile production and potteries. The valley was also the birthplace of iron railways. Wooden rails and horse-drawn wagons had been used to haul coal in the seventeenth century, but in 1729 the Coalbrookdale Company began casting iron wheels for railway wagons, and Richard Trevithick built his first steam locomotive at Coalbrookdale in 1802.

Allied Ironfounders Ltd, still in business on Abraham Darby's original site, was the only company of any size left, and in 1959, to celebrate the 250th anniversary of smelting by coke, they excavated the half-buried and almost forgotten Darby furnace. With town planners and developers eager to clear away the past, a group of enthusiasts persuaded the Telford Development Corporation to save the unique industrial monuments of a four-mile stretch of the valley. The Ironbridge Gorge Museum Trust was set up in 1967 and has continued the fascinating task of unravelling the story of the Industrial Revolution.

do not seem like strangers to us. Only 300 years separates us from them. Their portraits, their language and their monuments reflect the Englishness of a culture that had been forged over twelve and a half centuries and, if you disregard the wigs, the waistcoats and the breeches, the cast of their minds as revealed through their personal letters and books is not unlike our own. And the reason for this is surely history. Each of us is formed by our own family history, and in the same way, societies are fashioned by their collective experiences. And those early eighteenth-century English men and women shared a past with us: the Roman centuries; Saxon and Viking invasion; domination by a French-speaking aristocracy; traumas such as the Black Death, famine, war and religious persecution.

Tracing many of the influences and experiences that have shaped the English character, at Ironbridge Gorge we see the English about to embark on two centuries of industrialisation, trading and empire building. We can mark the start of that new direction in 1707 when Abraham Darby arrived in Coalbrookdale – the year of the Act of Union with Scotland. Queen Anne ceased to be queen of England and became queen of Great Britain. English history ends in 1707 and British history begins. Deep inside Abraham Darby's 'experimental laboratory', Jonathan and I had reached the end of our story of the English, though 5 metres of tunnel, rather than three centuries of time, separated us from late twentieth-century Britain and the futuristic pavilion which preserves the past of Ironbidge and presents it to the future as part of England's heritage.

Afterword

One of the most cherished English beliefs is that, being an island people, our history is radically different from that of our neighbours. Nothing could be further from the truth, for our experiences mirror those of the rest of Europe. Western Europeans had a common economy and culture. England's history, like that of many European states, began with the Germanic incursions into the Roman Empire, although it is true that the Anglo-Saxon settlement was more thorough and destructive than elsewhere. Many European peoples had to endure later invasions and for some there were centuries of domination by foreigners speaking another language. All Europe suffered catastrophically from the Black Death, from political instability and from civil wars; and all of northern Europe – and much of southern – shared in the upheavals that accompanied and followed the Reformation.

There is, however, no doubt that the 'European' experiences of the English resulted in a culture that was unique, just as from a similar past there emerged something recognisably French. The fact is that, although the ingredients in the recipe are the same, the quantities used and the method of cooking are slightly different in each case. Of the many special elements which affected our development, three spring to mind. First, England was geographically small enough for political debate to take place on a national stage. There came into being a national opposition to government and, in the precocious development of Parliament, a national forum; elsewhere, provincial assemblies and local political movements were of more significance. Secondly, the English language was strong enough to emerge from centuries underground and showed itself to be a superb cultural vehicle, particularly well suited to the adversarial nature of English politics and law. Thirdly, the Church of England after the Reformation, which at least in Elizabethan times had a theology little different from that prevailing in Geneva or Scotland, was dominated by pragmatic conformists, who seem to have inherited the practical, non-speculative strain already apparent in Anglo-Saxon thought and were prepared to tolerate divergences provided the forms were maintained. Conformity and an emphasis on continuity imposed on the English an approach to Church affairs which somehow managed to gloss over the traumatic break with the medieval past, giving the impression that the sixteenth-century revolution was not a revolution at all.

There emerged, therefore, a recognisably English culture and much of it survives today. But the global, extra-European attitudes of the British in the nineteenth century masked the fact that it was a variation on a European theme. In good things as well as in bad – and of course there are both – we are Europeans as well as being English.

JONATHAN RILEY-SMITH

Gazetteer of Sites

Chapter 1

West Stow Anglo-Saxon village: Suffolk. Located within a country park east of the A1101 between Bury St Edmunds and Mildenhall; visitors' centre and woodland nature trail. More information: The Visitors' Centre, West Stow Country Park, West Stow, Bury St Edmunds IP28 6HE.

Portchester Castle: Hampshire. North shore of Portsmouth Harbour, about 1 kilometre south of Portchester Station and the A27 Fareham to Chichester road. More information: English Heritage, Marketing Department, Keysign House, 49 Oxford St, London W1R 2HD.

Mausoleum of Galla Placidia: Ravenna, Italy; on the north Adriatic coast, south of Venice. The mausoleum shares the ancient city centre with a dozen or so fifth-century and late-Roman buildings. 74 kilometres by road or train from Bologna. More information: Azienda di Promozione Turistica della Provincia di Ravenna, Via San Vitale, 2, Ravenna, Italy.

Sutton Hoo Treasure: Early medieval room, British Museum, London.

St Martin's Church, Canterbury: Kent. East of city wall on the road to Sandwich, the A257, within view of the cathedral towers. More information: The Secretary, The Friends of St Martin's, 55 St Augustine's Road, Canterbury.

St Paul's Church, Jarrow: The church and monastic ruins lie just to the east of the southern entrance to the Tyne Tunnel. Exhibition in eighteenth-century Jarrow Hall includes artefacts from Bede's monastery. More information: Jarrow Hall, Church Bank, Jarrow, Tyne and Wear, or English Heritage (see address under Chapter 1 *Portchester Castle*).

Charlemagne's Palace Chapel: Aachen, Germany. At meeting point of German, Belgian and Dutch frontiers, 70 kilometres south-west of Cologne. More information: Dom zu Aachen, Aachen.

Chapter 2

Hedeby (Haithabu): Germany. On a Baltic inlet at the southern end of the Jutland Peninsula, on outskirts of Schleswig. Impressive eastern ramparts and adjacent museum. Finds from excavations, including Viking ships. More information: Wikinger Museum, Haithabu, Schleswig.

Jorvik Viking Centre: York; city centre location on Coppergate. Roman remains, medieval wall, city gates, and Viking reconstructions. More information: York Archaeological Trust, 47 Aldwark, York, YO1 2BY.

Wareham: Dorset. The A351 from Poole runs through the town at western extremity of Poole Harbour. More information: Purbeck Tourist Information Centre, Town Hall, Wareham, BH20 4NG.

Cheddar Palace: Somerset. Palace ground plan in the garden of Kings of Wessex School, Cheddar. B3135 via A38 and A371 from Bristol. More information: Taunton Museum, Taunton, Somerset.

Odda's Chapel: Deerhurst, Somerset. Saxon priory church and Odda's chapel within a few hundred metres of each other. Hamlet, in rural isolation, off B4213 Tewkesbury, 6 kilometres via A38. More information: English Heritage (see address under Chapter 1 *Portchester Castle*).

Bayeux: Normandy, France. Superb fifteenth-century cathedral. 27 kilometres from Caen. Tapestry imaginatively displayed in former bishop's palace. More information: Tapisserie de Bayeux, Rue Nesmond, Centre Culturel, Bayeux 14400.

Battle: Sussex. Battle Abbey, now a girls' school. Looks down on the town and battlefield, 11 kilometres from Hastings on A28. More information: English Heritage (see address under Chapter 1 *Portchester Castle*).

Chapter 3

Durham: County Durham. University city dominated by medieval castle and cathedral complex. Newcastle is 20 kilometres via A1(M) and A167. More information: Cathedral Bookshop, Durham Cathedral, County Durham.

Rievaulx Abbey: North Yorkshire. 3½ kilometres west of Helmsley, off B1257. More information: English Heritage (see address under Chapter 1 *Portchester Castle*).

Abbey of St Ruf: Avignon, Provence, France. Ruin in suburban public park. 1½ kilometres south of Porte St Michel via Avenue St Ruf, Avignon.

Canterbury Cathedral: Kent. Centrepiece of historic medieval walled town; Roman and monastic ruins, medieval city centre. 98 kilometres from London via M2/A2. More information: Dean and Chapter, Canterbury Cathedral, Canterbury.

Castle of Chinon: Loire Valley, France. Clifftop ruin overlooking town and tributary, River Vienne. 43 kilometres from Tours via D751. *Fontevraud Abbey* nearby, 4½ kilometres via D751 and N147. More information: Musée Archéologique, Ancienne Eglise et Château au 'Vieux Cravant', Cravant-les-Coteaux 37500.

Richmond Castle: North Yorkshire. Splendid eleventh- and twelfth-century ruin dominating small town. 38 kilometres from Middlesbrough via A1(M) and A6108. More information: English Heritage (see address under Chapter 1 *Portchester Castle*).

Chapter 4

Westminster Abbey: London. England's 'national' church, alongside Parliament and Whitehall ministries. Breathtaking royal mausoleum. More information: Abbey Bookshop, Westminster Abbey, London SW1.

Kenilworth Castle: Warwickshire. Acres of twelfth- and seventeenth-century ruins surrounded by pasture that was once the bed of a defensive lake. 29 kilometres from Birmingham via the A52 and A452. More information: English Heritage (see address under Chapter 1 *Portchester Castle*).

Stokesay Castle: Shropshire. Set in a valley and surrounded by hills. The county is rich in Roman, iron age and medieval sites. 35 kilometres from Shrewsbury via the A49; signposted 1¼ kilometres south of The Craven Arms. More information: English Heritage (see address under Chapter 1 *Portchester Castle*).

Chapter House, Westminster Abbey: London. Entrance through cloisters. Adjacent undercroft museum with superb death masks and effigies of medieval and later kings. More information: English Heritage (see address under Chapter 1 *Portchester Castle*).

Merton College: Oxford. Twelfth-century college quad in one of Oxford's 34 colleges. Entrance through an imposing sixteenth-century gatehouse in Merton Street. 90 kilometres north-west of London via A40 and A40(M). More information: Tourist Information Centre, Oxford.

Monpazier: South-west France. Founded by Edward I in 1285, it is a perfectly preserved fragment of English Gascony. Often packed with nostalgic Englishmen in Volvos who reach it by the D660 45 kilometres from Bergerac (Michelin Map 75).

More information: Syndicat d'Initiative, Monpazier, Dordogne.

Chapter 5

Laxton: Nottinghamshire. Medieval strip-farming in action. Rare survival of open fields and management system devised in the Middle Ages. Exhibition in outbuildings of village pub. Notable motte and bailey Norman castle and much altered medieval church. 16 kilometres from Newark-on-Trent via A1 or A616. More information: Laxton Visitors' Centre, Dovecote Inn, Laxton.

Ashwell Church: Hertfordshire. Black death graffiti scratched on church tower wall. Market town of the Middle Ages with many early buildings including a guildhall; a fifteenth-century house contains the village museum. 8 kilometres from Baldock via A1(M). More information: Ashwell Church, Ashwell.

Villandraut: South-west France. Moated ruined castle, seat of Pope Clement V and last of the 'English' castles to hold out in the 100 Years War. 57 kilometres from Bordeaux via A62, D11, D110 (Michelin map 234). More information: Syndicat d'Initiative du Canton de Villandraut, Villandraut.

Malbork Castle: Poland. Teutonic Knights headquarters. Vast brick built castle, much damaged during World War II, and still undergoing conservation. Gdansk is 62 kilometres across the Vistula Delta plain. More information: Castle Museum, Malbork.

Bolton Castle: North Yorkshire. Privately owned fourteenth-century pile that was slighted by Cromwell. Present owner gradually conserving the huge building and opening areas that have been closed for almost three centuries. More information: Bolton Castle, Leyburn, North Yorkshire.

Tewkesbury Abbey: Gloucestershire. The magnificent Abbey church contains many monuments to Tewkesbury's battle of 1471 in the Wars of the Roses. The so-called 'Bloody Meadow' is a short walk across open country and is marked by a notice on a field gate. 17 kilometres from Gloucester via A38. More information: Tourist Information Centre, Barton Street, Tewkesbury.

Chapter 6

Merchant Adventurers' Hall: York. Superb guildhall that dates from 1357; in a city that features an almost unbroken circuit of medieval city wall; a Norman castle and Viking and Roman archaeological remains 312 kilometres from London via A1 and A64. More information: Merchant Adventurers' Hall, Fossgate, York YO1 2XD.

St Cross: Hampshire. Medieval hospital established in 1156. Norman chapel, medieval Hall and fifteenth-century apartments for pensioners. Located on the fringe of Winchester about 5 kilometres from the city centre. More information: The Master, Hospital of St Cross, Winchester.

Lavenham: Suffolk. Entire streets of fifteenth-century houses plus two guildhalls and a towering medieval church. 25 kilometres from Ipswich via A1071 and A1141. More information: Tourist Information Centre, Lavenham.

Glastonbury Abbey: Somerset. Abbey ruins of what was once England's richest medieval monastery. Bristol 80 kilometres via M5 and A39. More information: Glastonbury Abbey, Glastonbury.

Queen's College: Cambridge. A fifteenth-century foundation where the famous Renaissance philosopher, Erasmus, spent several periods as a don. His room in the Erasmus tower is pointed out to visitors but special arrangements are needed to see the college's fifteenth-century library. Cambridge 88 kilometres from London via the M11. More information: The Keeper, The Old Library, Queen's College, Cambridge.

Wilton House: Wiltshire. Stately home of the Earls of Pembroke; stunning decor in the State apartments by Inigo Jones. Privately owned and situated 5 kilometres from Salisbury on the A30. More information: Wilton House, Wilton.

Lambeth Palace: London. Bishops of Canterbury's London base since the Middle Ages. Parts of the palace date from the thirteenth century and, along with the library, can be visited by appointment. More information: Lambeth Palace, Lambeth Palace Road, London SE1.

Chapter 7

Montacute House: Somerset. Late sixteenth-century mansion. Elizabethan plaster work plus a long gallery at the top of the house which now exhibits portraits of the period from the National Portrait Gallery. The village of Montacute is 15 kilometres from Yeovil via the A3088.

Newark Castle and *Queen's Sconce:* Nottinghamshire. Impressive ruined castle on Trent riverbank. Importance to Charles I's forces in the Civil War explained in town museum. Massive diamond shaped earthworks, *The Queen's Sconce*, on the outskirts of town where Royalists kept Roundheads at bay. Access via Carter Gate and Hawton Road. 175 kilometres from London via A1.

Banqueting House, Whitehall: London. The only remaining part of the old Whitehall Palace. Inigo Jones at his breathtaking best, and the venue for Charles I's execution in 1649. More information: Royal Palaces, Department of the Environment, 2 Marsham Street, London SW1P 3EB.

Burford Church: Oxfordshire. Delightful parish church with powerful Cromwellian associations. 25 kilometres from Oxford on A40. More information: The Vicarage, Burford Church, Burford, Oxford OX8 4SE.

Appleby Castle: Cumbria. Norman fortress rebuilt by Lady Anne Clifford in the 1650s. Also almshouses and the parish church in town. 22 kilometres from Penrith via A66. More information: Ferguson Industrial Holdings plc, Appleby Castle, Appleby, Cumbria.

Chapter 8

Royal Observatory: London. Situated in Greenwich Park overlooking the Thames. Built by Christopher Wren for the first Astronomer Royal in 1675; now a museum. About 10 kilometres downstream from London Bridge. More information: National Maritime Museum, Greenwich, London SE10.

Château of Saint-Germain-en-Laye: France. Louis XIV's massive palace (now a museum) in which James II took refuge after 1688. James's memorial is in the church opposite the castle entrance. Paris is 24 kilometres west along the Seine valley. More information: Musée des antiquités Nationales, Saint-Germain-en-Laye 78640.

Remonstrant Church: Amsterdam. Remarkable survival of seventeenth-century wooden church, not visible from the road, where English philosopher John Locke wrote and studied. One block from Anne Frank's famous house in central Amsterdam. Address and more information: Joh. A. Riesener, Keizersgracht 110, Amsterdam.

Royal Fort House: Bristol. Eighteenth-century Bristol merchant's mansion completed in 1760s. Now part of Bristol University, it can be visited only during August, 2pm–5pm weekdays. More information: Department of Music, University of Bristol, Bristol.

Ironbridge Gorge: Shropshire. Several miles of the Severn valley, packed with remains of the industrial revolution. The Ironbridge itself spans the river on the outskirts of Telford. 215 kilometres from London on M6 and M54. More information: The Ironbridge Gorge Museum, Ironbridge, Telford, Shropshire, TF8 7AW.

Bibliography

Chapter 1

CAMPBELL, J., *The Anglo-Saxons* Phaidon, 1982.

FRERE, S. S., *Britannia – History of Roman Britain* Routledge, 1987.

HUNTER-BLAIR, P., *The world of Bede* Cambridge University Press, 1990.

STENTON, F. M., *Anglo-Saxon England* (Ancient peoples and places) Oxford University Press, 1971; pbk., 1989.

THOMAS, C., *Celtic Britain* Thames and Hudson, 1986.

WEBB, J. F. & FARMER, D. H., (trans) *The age of Bede* (rev. ed. of *Lives of the saints*) Penguin, 1983.

WHITELOCK, D., *The beginnings of English society* Penguin, 1971.

Chapter 2

BARLOW, F., *Edward the Confessor* Eyre Methuen, 1979.

BROOKE, C. N. L., *The Saxon and Norman kings* Fontana, 1967.

CAMPBELL, J., *The Anglo-Saxons* Phaidon, 1982.

DOUGLAS, D. C., *William the Conqueror* (English monarchs) Eyre Methuen, 1977.

HALL, R., *The Viking dig: Excavations at York* Bodley Head, 1984.

KEYNES, S. & LAPIDGE, M. (ed), *Alfred the Great: Asser's 'Life of King Alfred' and other contemporary sources* Penguin, 1983.

LOYN, H. R., *The Vikings in Britain* Batsford, 1977. op.

SAWYER, P. H., *The age of the Vikings* E. Arnold, 1962; pbk., 1971. op.

STENTON, F. M., *Anglo-Saxon England* Oxford University Press, 1971; pbk., 1989.

WILSON, D. M., *The Bayeaux tapestry* Thames and Hudson, 1985. op.

Chapter 3

BARLOW, F., *Thomas a Becket* Weidenfeld and Nicolson, 1986; pbk., 1987.

CHIBNALL, M., *Anglo-Norman England, 1066–1166* Blackwell, 1987.

GILLINGHAM, J., *The Angevin empire* E. Arnold, 1984. op.

HIBBERT, C., *The English – a social history, 1066–1945* Grafton, 1987; pbk., 1988.

POOLE, A. L., *From Domesday Book to Magna Carta, 1087–1216* (Oxford history of England, Vol 3.) Oxford University Press, 1955.

SEYMOUR, W., *Battles in Britain* Sidgwick and Jackson, 1979; pbk., 1979.

WARREN, W. L., *Henry II* (English monarchs) Eyre Methuen, 1977.

Chapter 4

BARLOW, F., *Edward the Confessor* Eyre Methuen, 1979.

BUTT, R., *A history of Parliament – the Middle Ages* Constable, 1989.

COBBAN, A. B., *The medieval English universities – Oxford and Cambridge to c. 1500* Scolar Press, 1988.

LLOYD, T. H., *The English wool trade in the Middle Ages* Cambridge University Press, 1977. op.

PRESTWICH, M., *Edward I* Methuen, 1990.

PRESTWICH, M., *The three Edwards: war and state in England, 1272–1377* Methuen, 1981.

ROWLEY, T., *The high Middle Ages, 1200–1550* Routledge, 1986; Paladin Grafton, 1988.

Chapter 5

BOLTON, J. L., *The medieval English economy, 1150–1500* Dent, 1985.

CHRISTIANSEN, E., *The Northern crusade – the Baltic and the Catholic frontier, 1100–1525* Macmillan, 1980. op.

GILLINGHAM, J. B., *The Wars of the Roses* Weidenfeld and Nicolson, 1981; pbk., 1990.

HOUSLEY, N., *The Avignon papacy and the crusades, 1305–78* Oxford University Press, 1986.

HUSSEY, S. S., *Chaucer – an introduction* Methuen, 1981.

KEEN, M. H., *England in the later Middle Ages – a political history* Methuen, 1973. op.

PRESTWICH, M., *The three Edwards – War and state in England, 1272–1377* Methuen, 1981.

Chapter 6

CLAY, C. G. A., *Economic expansion and social change: England, 1500–1700* 2 Vols. Cambridge University Press, 1984.

CLAY, R. M., *The medieval hospitals of England* F. Cass, 1966.

GUY, J., *Tudor England* Oxford University Press, 1988; pbk., 1990.

HOSKINS, W. G., *The making of the English landscape* Penguin, 1985; Hodder and Stoughton, 1988.

REESE, M. M., *Shakespeare: his world and his work* E. Arnold, 1953, 1980; St Martin's Press, 1980. op.

SIMON, J., *Education and society in Tudor England* Cambridge University Press, 1979.

SMITH, A. G. R., *The emergence of a nation state* (Foundation of modern Britain) Longman, 1984.

Chapter 7

ACKROYD, P. R., et al. eds, *The Cambridge history of the Bible* 3 Vols. Combined vol., Cambridge University Press, 1988; individual vols., 1975–1976.

BRAILSFORD, H. N., *The Levellers and the English Revolution* Spokesman Books, 1976.

HILL, C., *God's Englishman – Oliver Cromwell and the English Revolution* Penguin, 1990.

HOLMES, M., *Proud Northern lady: Lady Anne Clifford, 1590–1676* Phillimore, 1976.

SMITH, A. G. R., *The emergence of a nation state* (Foundations of modern Britain) Longman, 1984.

STONE, L., *The causes of the English Revolution, 1529–1642* r.e. pbk., Ark Publications, 1986.

WEDGWOOD, C. V., *The trial of Charles I* Penguin, 1983.

Chapter 8

CLAY, C. G. A., *Economic expansion and social change – England, 1500–1700* 2 vols. Cambridge University Press, 1984.

COSSONS, N., *Industrial archaeology* David and Charles, 1969. op.

COWARD, B., *The Stuart age* Longman, 1980.

DUNN, J., *Locke* (Past masters) Oxford University Press, 1984.

DUNN, R. S., *Sugar and slaves – rise of the planter class in the English West Indies, 1624–1713* W. W. Norton, 1980.

FINBERG, H. P. R. ed, *The agrarian history of England and Wales* 4 Vols. Cambridge University Press, 1967; 1972. op.

GREGG, P., *Black Death to Industrial Revolution: a social and economic history* Harrap, 1976. op.

QUINN, D. B. & RYAN, A. N., *England's seas empire* Allen and Unwin, 1984.

Index

Picture Credits